The Poetry Of James Beattie

James Beattie was born on October 25th, 1735 at Laurencekirk in the Mearns in Scotland.

In 1749 James began his studies at Marischal College, Aberdeen. In 1753, he was awarded an MA degree. He then spent several years as a schoolteacher and briefly contemplated becoming a minister.

At only 25, he was, in 1760, appointed Professor of moral philosophy at Aberdeen University.

Later that year he published his first volume of poems 'Original Poems And Translations'. In 1765 he published The Judgment of Paris, which attracted much attention. However two further works were to gain him widespread fame. The first, published in 1770, was an essay – 'An Essay on the Nature and Immutability of Truth'. Intended as an answer to David Hume, this had great immediate success, and led to an introduction to the King, a pension of £200, and the degree of LL.D. from Oxford.

In 1771 he published the first book of 'The Minstrel' and the second in 1774. These two volumes set his place in literary history.

A noted abolitionist he was prominent in his argument in the aforementioned 'Essay on the Nature and Immutability of Truth (1770) and Elements of Moral Science.

A gifted amateur cellist and member of the Aberdeen Musical Society. He considered questions of music philosophy in his essay 'On Poetry and Music'

With the death of his wife and two sons his health and spirits were broken and he died in on August 18th 1803 aged 67 in Aberdeen.

Index Of Poems

Ode To Peace

I. I.

Peace, heaven-descended maid! whose powerful voice
From ancient darkness call'd the morn;
And hush'd of jarring elements the noise,
When Chaos, from his old dominion torn,
With all his bellowing throng,
Far, far was hurl'd the void abyss along;
And all the bright angelic choir,
Striking, through all their ranks, the eternal lyre,
Pour'd, in loud symphony, the impetuous strain;
And every fiery orb and planet sung,
And wide, through Night's dark solitary reign,
Rebounding long and deep, the lays triumphant rung!

I. II.

Oh, whither art thou fled, Saturnian Age!
Roll round again, majestic years!
To break the sceptre of tyrannic rage;
From Woe's wan cheek to wipe the bitter tears;
Ye years, again roll round!
Hark! from afar what desolating sound,
While echoes load the sighing gales,
With dire presage the throbbing heart assails!
Murder, deep-roused, with all the whirl wind's haste,
And roar of tempest, from her cavern springs,
Her tangled serpents girds around her waist,
Smiles ghastly fierce, and shakes her gore-distilling wings.

I. III.

The shouts, redoubling, rise
In thunder to the skies;
The nymphs disordered, dart along,
Sweet powers of solitude and song,
Stunn'd with the horros of discordant sound;
And all is listening, trembling round.
Torrents, far heard amid the waste of night,
That oft have led the wanderer right,
Are silent at the noise.
The mighty Ocean's more majestic voice,
Drown'd in superior din, is heard no more;

The surge in silence seems to sweep the foamy shore.

II. I.
The bloody banner, streaming in the air,
Seen on yon sky-mix'd mountain's brow,
The mingling multitudes, the madding car,
Driven in confusion to the plain below,
War's dreadful Lord proclaim.
Bursts out, by frequent fits, the expansive flame;
Snatch'd in tempestuous eddies, flies
The surging smoke o'er all the darken'd skies;
The cheerful face of heaven no more is seen;
The bloom of morning of morning fades to deadly pale;
The bat flies transient o'er the dusky green,
And Night's foul birds along the sullen twilight sail.

II. II.
Involved in fire-streak'd gloom, the car comes on,
The rushing steeds grim Terror guides,
His forehead writhed to a relentless frown,
Aloft the angry Power of Battles rides.
Grasped in his mighty hand
A mace tremendous desolates the land;
The tower rolls headlong down the steep,
The mountain shrinks before its wasteful sweep,
Chill horror the dissolving limbs invades,
Smit by the blasting lightning of his eyes;
A deeper gloom invests the howling shades;
Stripp'd is the shatter'd grove, and every verdure dies.

II. III.
How startled Phrenzy stares,
Bristling her ragged hairs!
Revenge the gory fragment gnaws;
See, with her griping vulture claws
Imprinted deep, she rends the mangled wound!
Hate whirls her torch sulphureous round.
The shrieks of agony, and clang of arms,
Re-echo to the hoarse alarms,
Her trump terrific blows.
Disparting from behind, the clouds disclose,
Of kingly gesture, a gigantic form,
That with his scourge sublime rules the careering storm.

III. I.
Ambition, outside fair! within as foul
As fiends of fiercest heart below,
Who rides the hurricanes of fire, that roll
Their thundering vortex o'er the realms of wo,

Yon naked waste survey;
Where late was heard the flute's mellifluous lay;
Where late the rosy-bosom'd hours,
In loose array, danced lightly o'er the flowers;
Where late the shepherd told his tender tale;
And, waken'd by the murmuring breeze of morn,
The voice of cheerful Labour fill'd the dale;
And dove-eyed Plenty smiled, and waved her liberal horn.

III. II.
Yon ruins, sable from the wasting flame,
But mark the once resplendent dome;
The frequent corse obstructs the sullen stream
And ghosts glare horrid from the sylvan gloom.
How sadly silent all!
Save where, outstretch'd beneath yon hanging wall
Pale Famine moans with feeble breath,
And Anguish yells, and grinds his bloody teeth.
Though vain the muse, and every melting lay
To touch thy heart, unconscious of remorse!
Know, monster, know, thy hour is on the way;
I see, I see the years begin their mighty course.

III. III.
What scenes of glory rise
Before my dazzled eyes!
Young zephyrs wave their wanton wings
And melody celestial rings.
All blooming on the lawn the nymphs advance,
And touch the lute, and range the dance:
And the blithe shepherds, on the mountain's side,
Array'd in all their rural pride,
Exalt the festive note,
Inviting Echo from her inmost grot
But ah! the landscape glows with fainter light;
It darkens, swims and flies for ever from my sight.

IV. I.
Illusions vain! Can sacred
Peace reside
Where sordid gold the breast alarms,
Where Cruelty inflames the eye of Pride,
And Grandeur wantons in soft Pleasure's arms!
Ambition, these are thine!
These from the soul erase the form divine;
And quench the animating fire,
That warms the bosom with sublime desire.
Thence the relentless heart forgets to feel,
And Hatred triumphs on the o'erwhelming brow,
And midnight Rancour grasps the cruel steel;

Blaze the blue flames of death, and sound the shrieks of wo.

IV. II.
From Albion fled, thy once beloved retreat,
What regions brighten in thy smile,
Creative
Peace! and underneath thy feet
See sudden flowers adorn the rugged soil?
In bleak Siberia blows,
Waked by the genial breath, the balmy rose?
Waved over by the magic wand,
Does life inform fell Lybia's burning sand?
O does some isle thy parting flight detain,
Where roves the Indian through primaeval shades
Haunts the pure pleasures of the sylvan reign,
And, led by Reason's light, the path of Nature treads?

IV. III.
On Cuba's utmost steep,
Far leaning o'er the deep,
The Goddess' pensive form was seen;
Her robe, of Nature's varied green,
Waved on the gale; grief dimm'd her radiant eyes;
Her bosom heaved with boding sighs;
She eyed the main, where, gaining on the view,
Emerging from the ethereal blue,
'Midst the dread of pomp of war,
Blazed the Iberian streamer from afar.
She saw; and, on refulgent pinions borne
Slow wing'd her way sublime, and mingled with the morn.

An Epitaph
Like thee I once have stemm'd the sea of life,
Like thee have languish'd after empty joys,
Like thee have labour'd in the stormy strife,
Been grieved for trifles, and amused with toys.

Forget my frailties; thou art also frail:
Forgive my lapses; for thyself may'st fall:
Nor read unmoved my artless tender tale

Elegy
I
Tired with the busy crowds, that all the day
Impatient throng where Folly's altars flame,
My languid powers dissolve with quick decay,
Till genial Sleep repair the sinking frame.

II

Hail, kind reviver! that canst lull the cares,
And every weary sense compose to rest,
Lighten the oppressive load which anguish bears,
And warm with hope the cold desponding breast.

III

Touch'd by thy rod, from Power's majestic brow
Drops the gay plume; he pines a lowly clown;
And on the cold earth stretch'd, the son of Woe
Quaffs Pleasure's draught, and wears a fancied crown.

IV

When roused by thee, on boundless pinions borne,
Fancy to fairy scenes exults to rove,
Now scales the cliff gay-gleaming on the morn,
Now sad and silent treads the deepening grove;

V

Or skims the main, and listens to the storms,
Marks the long waves roll far remote away;
Or, mingling with ten thousand glittering forms,
Floats on the gale, and basks in purest day.

VI

Haply, ere long, pierced by the howling blast,
Through dark and pathless deserts I shall roam,
Plunge down the unfathom'd deep, or shrink aghast
Where bursts the shrieking spectre from the tomb:

VII

Perhaps loose Luxury's enchanting smile
Shall lure my steps to some romantic dale,
Where Mirth's light freaks the unheeded hours beguile,
And airs of rapture warble in the gale.

VIII

Instructive emblem of this mortal state!
Where scenes as various every hour arise
In swift succession, which the hand of Fate
Presents, then snatches from our wondering eyes.

IX

Be taught, vain man, how fleeting all thy joys,
Thy boasted grandeur and thy glittering store:
Death comes, and all thy fancied bliss destroys;
Quick as a dream it fades, and is no more.

X

And, sons of Sorrow! though the threatening storm

Of angry Fortune overhang awhile,
Let not her frowns your inward peace deform;
Soon happier days in happier climes shall smile.

XI
Through Earth's throng'd visions while we toss forlorn,
'Tis tumult all, and rage, and restless strife;
But these shall vanish like the dreams of morn,
When Death awakes us to immortal life.

Ode To Hope
I. I.
O Thou, who glad'st the pensive soul,
More than Aurora's smile the swain forlorn,
Left all night long to mourn
Where desolation frowns, and tempests howl;
And shrieks of wo, as intermits the storm,
Far o'er the monstrous wilderness resound,
And cross the gloom darts many a shapeless form,
And many a fire-eyed visage glares around.
O come, and be once more my guest.
And oft with smiles indulgent cheer'd
And soothed him into rest.

I. II.
Smit by thy rapture-beaming eye
Deep flashing through the midnight of their mind,
The sable bands combined,
Where Fear's black banner bloats the troubled sky,
Appall'd retire. Suspicion hides her head,
Nor dares th' obliquely gleaming eyeball raise,
Despair, with gorgon-figured veil o'erspread,
Speeds to dark Phlegethon's detested maze.
Lo, startled at the heavenly ray,
With speed unwonted Indolence upsprings,
And, heaving, lifts her leaden wings,
And sullen glides away;

I. III.
Ten thousand forms, by pining Fancy view'd,
Dissolve - Above the sparkling flood
When Phoebus rears his awful brow,
From lengthening lawn and volley low
The troops of fen-born mists retire.
Along the plain
The joyous swain
Eyes the gay villages again,
And gold-illuminated spire
While on the billowy ether borne

Floats loose lay's jovial measure;
And light along the fairy Pleasure,
Her green robes glittering to the morn,
Wantons on silken wing. And goblins all
To the damp dungeon shrink, or hoary hall,
Or westward, with impetuous flight,
Shoot to the desert realms of their congenial Night.

II. I.
When first on Childhood's eager gaze
Life's varied landscape, stretch'd immense around,
Starts out of night profound,
Thy voice incites to tempt th' untrodden maze,
Fond he surveys thy mild maternal face,
His bashful eye still kindling as he views,
And, while thy lenient arm supports his pace,
With beating heart the upland path pursues?
The path that leads, where, hung sublime,
And seen afar, youth's gallant trophies, bright
In fancy's rainbow ray, invite
His wingy nerves to climb.

II. II.
Pursue thy pleasurable way,
Safe in the guidance of thy heavenly guard,
While melting airs are heard,
And soft-eyed cherub forms around thee play
Simplicity, in careless flowers array'd,
Prattling amusive in his accent meek;
And modesty, half turning as afraid,
The smile just dimpling on his glowing cheek!
Content and Leisure, hand in hand
With innocence and Peace, advance, and sing
And Mirth, in many a mazy ring,
Frisks o'er the flowery land.

II. III.
Frail man, how various is thy lot below!
To-day tho' gales propitious blow,
And Peace soft gliding down the sky
Lead Love along and Harmony,
To-morrow the gay scene deforms:
Then all around
The thunder's sound
Rolls rattling on through heaven's profound,
And down rush all the storms.
Ye days, that balmy influence shed,
When sweet Childhood, ever sprightly,
In paths of pleasure sported lightly,
Whither, ah whither are ye fled!

Ye cherub train, that brought him on his way,
O leave him not midst tumult and dismay;
For now youth's eminence he gains:
But what a weary length of lingering toil remains!

III. I.
They shrink, they vanish into air,
Now slander taints with pestilence the gale;
And mingling cries assail,
The wail of Wo, and groan of grim Despair.
Lo, wizard Envy from his serpent eye
Darts quick destruction in each baleful glance;
Pride smiling stern, and yellow Jealousy,
Frowning Disdain, and haggard Hate advance;
Behold, amidst the dire array,
Pale wither'd Care his giant-stature rears,
And lo, his iron hand prepares
To grasp its feeble prey.

III. II.
Who now will guard bewilder'd youth
Safe from the fierce assault of hostile rage!
Such war can Virtue wage,
Alas! full oft on Guilt's victorious car
The spoils of Virtue are in triumph borne;
While the fair captive, mark'd with many a scar
In lone obscurity, oppress'd, forlorn,
Resigns to tears her angel form.
Ill-fated youth, then whither wilt thou fly!
No friend, no shelter now is nigh,
And onward rolls the storm.

III. III.
But whence the sudden beam that shoots along?
Why shrink aghast the hostile throng?
Lo, from amidst Affliction's night,
Hope bursts all radiant on the sight;
Her words the troubled bosom sooth.
'Why thus dismay'd?
Though foes invade,
Hope ne'er is wanting to their aid,
'Tis I who smooth the rugged way,
I, who close the eyes of sorrow,
And with glad visions of to-morrow
Repair the weary soul's decay.
When Death's cold touch thrills to the freezing heart,
Dreams of heaven's opening glories I impart,
Till the freed spirit springs on high
In rapture too severe for weak mortality.'

Hope Beyond The Grave

'Tis night, and the landscape is lovely no more;
I mourn, but, ye woodlands, I mourn not for you;
For morn is approaching, your charms to restore,
Perfumed with fresh fragrance, and glittering with dew:
Nor yet for the ravage of winter I mourn;
Kind Nature the embryo blossom will save,
But when shall spring visit the mouldering urn!
O when shall day dawn on the night of the grave!

'Twas thus, by the glare of false science betray'd,
That leads, to bewilder; and dazzles, to blind;
My thoughts wont to roam, from shade onward to shade,
Destruction before me, and sorrow behind.
O pity, great Father of light, then I cried,
Thy creature, who fain would not wander from Thee;
Lo, humbled in dust, I relinquish'd my pride:
From doubt and from darkness Thou only canst free.

And darkness and doubt are now flying away,
No longer I roam in conjecture forlorn,
So breaks on the traveller, faint, and astray,
The bright and the balmy effulgence of morn.
See Truth, Love, and Mercy in triumph descending,
And Nature all glowing in Eden's first bloom!
On the cold cheek of Death smiles and roses are blending,
And beauty immortal awakes from the tomb.

Elegy (Tir'd With The Busy Crowds)

Tir'd with the busy crouds, that all the day
Impatient throng where Folly's altars flame,
My languid powers dissolve with quick decay,
Till genial Sleep repair the sinking frame.

Hail kind Reviver! that canst lull the cares,
And every weary sense compose to rest,
Lighten th' oppressive load which Anguish bears,
And warm with hope the cold desponding breast.

Touch'd by thy rod, from Power's majestic brow
Drops the gay plume; he pines a lowly clown;
And on the cold earth stretch'd the son of Woe
Quaffs Pleasure's draught, and wears a fancy'd crown.

When rous'd by thee, on boundless pinions born
Fancy to fairy scenes exults to rove,
Now scales the cliff gay-gleaming on the morn,

Now sad and silent treads the deepening grove;

Or skims the main, and listens to the storms,
Marks the long waves roll far remote away;
Or mingling with ten thousand glittering forms
Floats on the gale, and basks in purest day.

Haply, ere long, pierc'd by the howling blast
Through dark and pathless desarts I shall roam,
Plunge down th' unfathom'd deep, or shrink aghast
Where bursts the shrieking spectre from the tomb:

Perhaps loose Luxury's enchanting smile
Shall lure my steps to some romantic dale,
Where Mirth's light freaks th' unheeded hours beguile,
And airs of rapture warble in the gale.

Instructive emblem of this mortal state!
Where scenes as various every hour arise
In swift succession, which the hand of Fate
Presents, then snatches from our wondering eyes.

Be taught, vain man, how fleeting all thy joys,
Thy boasted grandeur, and thy glittering store;
Death comes, and all thy fancy'd bliss destroys,
Quick as a dream it fades, and is no more.

And, sons of Sorrow! though the threatening storm
Of angry Fortune overhang a while,
Let not her frowns your inward peace deform;
Soon happier days in happier climes shall smile.

Through earth's throng'd visions while we toss forlorn,
'Tis tumult all, and rage, and restless strife;
But these shall vanish like the dreams of morn,
When Death awakes us to immortal life.

Elegy. Written in 1758
Still, shall unthinking man substantial deem
The forms that fleet through life's deceitful dream?
On clouds, where Fancy's beam amusive plays,
Shall heedless Hope the towering fabric raise?
Till at Death's touch the fairy visions fly,
And real scenes rush dismal on the eye;
And from Elysium's balmy slumber torn
The startled soul awakes, to think and mourn.

O ye, whose hours in jocund train advance,
Whose spirits to the song of gladness dance,

Who flowery vales in endless view survey
Glittering in beams of visionary day;
O, yet while Fate delays th' impending wo,
Be roused to thought, anticipate the blow;
Lest, like the lightning's glance, the sudden ill
Flash to confound, and penetrate to kill;
Lest, thus encompass'd with funereal gloom,
Like me, ye bend o'er some untimely tomb,
Pour your wild ravings in Night's frighted ear,
And half pronounce Heavens sacred doom severe.

Wise, beauteous, good! O every grace combined,
That charms the eye, or captivates the mind!
Fair as the floweret opening on the morn,
Whose leaves bright drops of liquid pearl adorn!
Sweet, as the downy-pinion'd gale, that roves
To gather fragrance in Arabian groves!
Mild, as the strains, that, at the close of day
Warbling remote, along the vales decay!
Yet, why with these compared? What tints so fine
What sweetness, mildness, can be match'd with thine?
Why roam abroad? Since still, to fancy's eyes,
I see, I see thy lovely form arise.
Still let me gaze, and every care beguile,
Gaze on that cheek, where all the Graces smile;
That soul-expressing eye, benignly bright,
Where meekness beams ineffable delight;
That brow, where Wisdom sits enthroned serene,
Each feature forms, and dignifies the mien:
Still let me listen, while her words impart
The sweet effusions of the blameless heart,
Till all my soul, each tumult charm'd away,
Yields, gently led, to Virtue's easy sway.

By thee inspired, O Virtue, age is young,
And music warbles from the faltering tongue:
Thy ray creative cheers the clouded brow,
And decks the faded cheek with rosy glow,
Brightens the joyless aspect, and supplies
Pure heavenly lustre to the languid eyes;
But when Youth's living bloom reflects thy beams,
Resistless on the view the glory streams,
Love, Wonder, Joy, alternately alarm,
And Beauty dazzles with angelic charm.

Ah whither fled! - ye dear illusions stay
Lo, pale and silent lies the lovely clay.
How are the roses on that cheek decay'd,
Which late the purple light of youth display'd!
Health on her form each sprightly grace bestow'd;
With life and thought each speaking feature glow'd

Fair was the flower, and soft the vernal sky;
Elate with hope, we deem'd no tempest nigh;
When lo, a whirlwind's instantaneous gust
Left all its beauties withering in the dust.

All cold the hand, that soothed Wo's weary head!
And quench'd the eye, the pitying tear that shed!
And mute the voice, whose pleasing accents stole,
Infusing balm, into the rankled soul!
O Death, why arm with cruelty thy power,
And spare the idle weed, yet lop the flower!
Why fly thy shafts in lawless error driven!
Is Virtue then no more the care of Heaven!
But peace, bold thought! be still my bursting heart!
We, not Eliza , felt the fatal dart.
'Scaped the dark dungeon does the slave complain,
Nor bless the hand that broke the galling chain?
Say, pines not Virtue for the lingering morn,
On this dark wild condemn'd to roam forlorn?
Where Reason's meteor-rays, with sickly glow,
O'er the dun gloom a dreadful glimmering flow?
Disclosing dubious to th' affrighted eye
O'erwhelming mountains tottering from on high,
Black billowy seas in storm perpetual toss'd,
And weary ways in wildering labyrinths lost.
O happy stroke that bursts the bonds of clay,
Darts through the rending gloom the blaze of day,
And wings the soul with boundless flight to soar,
Where dangers threat, and fears alarm no more.

Transporting thought! here let me wipe away
The tear of grief, and wake a bolder lay.
But ah! the swimming eye o'erflows anew,
Nor check the sacred drops to pity due;
Lo, where in speechless, hopeless anguish, bend
O'er her loved dust, the Parent, Brother, Friend!
How vain the hope of man! - But cease thy strain,
Nor Sorrow's dread solemnly profane;
Mix'd with yon drooping Mourners, on her bier
In silence shed the sympathetic tear.

The Hermit

At the close of day, when the hamlet is still,
And mortals the sweets of forgetfulness prove,
When nought but the torrent is heard on the hill,
And nought but the nightingale's song in the grove.
'Twas thus, by the cave of the mountain afar,
While his harp rung symphonious, a Hermit began
No more with himself or with nature at war,

He thought as a Sage, though he felt as a Man.

'Ah, why, all abandon'd to darkness and wo,
Why, lone Philomela, that languishing fall?
For Spring shall return, and a lover bestow,
But, if pity inspire thee, renew the sad lay,
Mourn, sweetest complainer, man calls thee to mourn;
O soothe him, whose pleasures like thine pass away
Full quickly they pass - but they never return.

'Now gliding remote, on the verge of the sky,
The Moon, half-extinguish'd, her crescent displays:
But lately I mark'd, when majestic on high
She shone, and the planets were lost in her blaze.
Roll on, thou fair orb, and with gladness pursue
The path that conducts thee to splendour again.
But Man's faded glory what change shall renew!
Ah fool! to exult in a glory so vain!

''Tis night, and the landscape is lovely no more;
I mourn, but, ye woodlands, I mourn not for you;
For morn is approaching, your charms to restore,
Perfumed with fresh fragrance, with glittering dew,
Nor yet for the ravage of winter I mourn;
Kind Nature the embryo blossom will save.
But when shall Spring visit the mouldering urn!
O when shall it dawn on the night of the grave!

''Twas thus, by the glare of false Science betray'd,
That leads, to bewilder; and dazzles, to blind;
My thoughts wont to roam, from shade onward to shade,
Destruction before me, and sorrow behind.
'O pity, great Father of light,' then I cried,
'Thy creature who fain would not wander from Thee!
Lo, humbled in dust, I relinquish my pride:
From doubt and from darkness thou only canst free.

'And darkness and doubt are now flying away,
No longer I roam in conjecture forlorn.
So breaks on the traveller, faint, and astray,
The bright and the balmy effulgence of morn.
see Truth, Love, and Mercy, in triumph descending,
And Nature all glowing in Eden's first bloom!
On the cold cheek of Death smiles and roses are blending,
And Beauty Immortal awakes from the tomb.'

Epistle To The Honourable C. B.
When B*** invites me, and inviting sings,
Instant I'd fly, (had heaven vouchsafed me wings)

To hail him in that calm sequestered seat,
Whence he looks down with pity on the great;
And, midst the groves retired, at leisure wooes
Domestic love, contentment, and the Muse.
I wish for wings and winds to speed my course;
Since B--t and the fates refuse a horse.
Where now the Pegasus of antient time,
And Ippogrifo famed in modern rhime?
O, where that wooden steed, whose every leg
Like lightning flew, obsequious to the peg;
The waxen wings by Daedalus designed,
And China waggons wafted by the wind?
A Spaniard reached the moon, upborn by geese;
(Then first 'twas known that she was made of cheese.)
A fidler on a fish through waves advanced,
He twanged his catgut, and the Dolphin danced.
Hags rode on broom-sticks, heathen-gods on clouds;
Ladies, on rams and bulls, have dared the floods.
Much famed the shoes Jack Giant-killer wore,
And Fortunatus' hat is famed much more.
Such vehicles were common once, no doubt;
But modern versemen must even trudge on foot,
Or doze at home, expectants of the gout.
Hard is the task, indeed 'tis wondrous hard,
To act the Hirer, yet preserve the Bard.
'Next week, by, (but 'tis a sin to swear)
'I give my word, sir, you shall have my mare;
'Sound wind and limb, as any ever was,
'And rising only seven years old next grass.
'Four miles an hour she goes, nor needs a spur;
'A pretty piece of flesh, upon my conscience, sir.'
This speech was B--t's; and, tho' mean in phrase,
The nearest thing to prose, as Horace says,
(Satire the fourth, and forty-second line)
'Twill intimate that I propose to dine
Next week with B***. Muse, lend thine aid a while;
For this great purpose claims a lofty style.
Ere yonder sun, now glorious in the west,
Has thrice three times reclined on Thetis' breast;
Ere thrice three times, from old Tithonus' bed,
Her charms all glowing with celestial red,
The balmy morn shall rise to mortal view,
And from her bright locks shake the pearls of dew,
These eyes, O B***, shall hail thy opening glades,
These ears shall catch the music of thy shades;
This cherished frame shall drink the gladsome gales,
And the fresh fragrance of thy flowery vales.
And (for I know the Muse will come along)
To B*** I mean to meditate a song:
A song, adorned with every rural charm,
Trim as thy garden, ample as thy farm,

Sweet as thy milk, and brisk as bottled beer,
Wholesome as mutton, and as water clear,
In wildflowers fertile, as thy fields of corn,
And frolicksome as lambs, or sheep new shorn.
I ask not ortolans, or Chian wine,
The fat of rams, or quintessence of swine.
Her spicy stores let either India keep,
Nor El Dorado vend her golden sheep.
And to the mansion house, or council hall,
Still on her black splay feet may the huge tortoise crawl.
Not Parson's butt my appetite can move,
Nor, Bell, thy beer; nor even thy nectar, Jove.
If B*** be happy, and in health, his guest,
Whom wit and learning charm, can wish no better feast.

The Hares, A Fable

Yes, yes, I grant the sons of earth
Are doom'd to trouble from their birth.
We all of sorrow have our share;
But say, is yours without compare?
Look round the world; perhaps you'll find
Each individual of our kind
Press'd with an equal load of ill,
Equal at least. Look further still,
And own your lamentable case
Is little short of happiness.
In yonder hut that stands alone
Attend to Famine's feeble moan;
Or view the couch where Sickness lies,
Mark his pale cheek, and languid eyes,
His frame by strong convulsion torn,
His struggling sighs, and looks forlorn.
Or see, transfix'd with keener pangs,
Where o'er his hoard the miser hangs;
Whistles the wind; he starts, he stares,
Nor Slumber's balmy blessing shares,
Despair, Remorse, and Terror roll
Their tempests on his harass'd soul.

But here perhaps it may avail
T'enforce our reasoning with a tale.

Mild was the morn, the sky serene,
The jolly hunting band convene,
The beagle's breast with ardour burns,
The bounding steed the champaign spurns,
And Fancy oft the game descries
Through the hound's nose, and huntsman's eyes.

Just then, a council of the hares
Had met, on national affairs.
The chiefs were set; while o'er their head
The furze its frizzled covering spread.
Long lists of grievances were heard,
And general discontent appear'd,
'Our harmless race shall every savage
Both quadruped and biped ravage?
Shall horses hounds and hunters still
Unite their wits to work us ill?
The youth, his parent's sole delight,
Whose tooth the dewy lawns invite,
Whose pulse in every vein beats strong,
Whose limbs leap light the vales along,
May yet ere noontide meet his death,
And lie dismember'd on the heath.
For youth, alas, nor cautious age,
Nor strength, nor speed, eludes their rage.
In every field we meet the foe,
Each gale comes fraught with sounds of wo;
The morning but awakes our fears,
The evening sees us bathed in tears.
But must we ever idly grieve,
Nor strive our fortunes to relieve?
Small is each individual's force:
To stratagem be our recourse;
And then, from all our tribes combined,
The murderer to his cost may find
No foes are weak, whom Justice arms,
Whom Concord leads, and Hatred warms.
Be roused; or liberty acquire,
Or in the great attempt expire.'
He said no more, for in his breast
Conflicting thoughts the voice suppress'd:
The fire of vengeance seem'd to stream
From his swoln eyeball's yellow gleam.

And now the tumults of the war,
Mingling confusedly from afar,
Swell in the wind. Now louder cries
Distinct of hounds and men arise.
Forth from the brake, with beating heart
Th' assembled hares tumultuous start,
And, every straining nerve on wing,
Away precipitately spring.
The hunting band, a signal given,
Thick thundering o'er the plain are driven;
O'er cliff abrupt, and shrubby mound,
And river broad, impetuous bound;
Now plunge amid the forest shades,
Glance through the openings of the glades;

Now o'er the level valley sweep,
Now with short steps strain up the steep;
While backward from the hunter's eyes
The landscape like a torrent flies.
At last an ancient wood they gain'd,
By pruner's axe yet unprofaned,
High o'er the rest, by Nature rear'd,
The oak's majestic boughs appear'd;
Beneath, a copse of various hue
In barbarous luxuriance grew.
No knife had curb'd the rambling sprays,
No hand had wove th' implicit maze.
The flowering thorn, self-taught to wind,
The hazle's stubborn stem entwined,
And bramble twigs were wreathed around,
And rough furze crept along the ground.
Here sheltering, from the sons of murther,
The hares drag their tired limbs no further.

But lo, the western wind erelong
Was loud, and roar'd the woods among;
From rustling leaves, and crashing boughs,
The sound of wo and war arose.
The hares distracted scour the grove,
As terror and amazement drove;
But danger, wheresoe'er they fled,
Still seem'd impending o'er their head.
Now crowded in a grotto's gloom,
All hope extinct, they wait their doom.
Dire was the silence, till, at length,
Even from despair deriving strength,
With bloody eye, and furious look,
A daring youth arose, and spoke.

'O wretched race, the scorn of Fate,
Whom ills of every sort await!
O, cursed with keenest sense to feel
The sharpest sting of every ill!
Say ye, who, fraught with mighty scheme,
Of liberty and vengeance dream,
What now remains? To what recess
Shall we our weary steps address,
Since fate is evermore pursuing
All ways, and means to work our ruin?
Are we alone, of all beneath,
Condemn'd to misery worse than death!
Must we, with fruitless labour, strive
In misery worse than death to live!
No. Be the smaller ill our choice:
So dictates Nature's powerful voice.
Death's pang will in a moment cease;

And then, All hail, eternal peace!'
Thus while he spoke, his words impart
The dire resolve to every heart.
A distant lake in prospect lay,
That glittering in the solar ray,
Gleam'd through the dusky trees, and shot
A trembling light along the grott.
Thither with one consent they bend,
Their sorrows with their lives to end,
While each, in thought, already hears
The water hissing in his ears.

Fast by the margin of the lake,
Conceal'd within a thorny brake,
A Linnet sat, whose careless lay
Amused the solitary day,
Careless he sung, for on his breast
Sorrow no lasting trace impress'd;
When suddenly he heard a sound
Of swift feet traversing the ground.
Quick to the neighbouring tree he flies,
Thence trembling cast around his eyes;
No foe appear'd, his fears were vain;
Pleased he renews the sprightly strain.

The hares, whose noise had caused his fright,
Saw with surprise the linnet's flight.
Is there on earth a wretch, they said,
Whom our approach can strike with dread?
An instantaneous change of thought
To tumult every bosom wrought.
So fares the system-building sage,
Who, plodding on from youth to age,
At last on some foundation-dream
Has rear'd aloft his goodly scheme,
And proved his predecessors fools,
And bound all nature by his rules;
So fares he in that dreadful hour,
When injured Truth exerts her power
Some new phenomenon to raise;
Which, bursting on his frighted gaze,
From its proud summit to the ground
Proves the whole edifice unsound.

'Children,' thus spoke a hare sedate,
Who oft had known th' extremes of fate,
'In slight events docile mind
May hints of good instruction find.
That our condition is the worst,
And we with such misfortunes cursed
As all comparison defy,

Was late the universal cry.
When lo, an accident so slight
As yonder little linnet's flight,
Has made your stubborn heart confess
(So your amazement bids me guess)
That all our load of woes and fears
Is but a part of what he bears.
Where can he rest secure from harms,
Whom even a helpless hare alarms?
Yet he repines not at his lot,
When pass'd the danger is forgot;
On yonder bough he trims his wings,
And with unusual rapture stings;
While we, less wretched, sink beneath
Our lighter ills, and rush to death.
No more of this unmeaning rage,
But hear, my friends, the words of age.

'When by the winds of autumn driven
The scatter'd clouds fly cross the heaven,
Oft have we, from some mountain's head,
Beheld th' alternate light and shade
Sweep the long vale. Here hovering lours
The shadowy cloud; there downward pours,
Streaming direct, a flood of day,
Which from the view flies swift away;
It flies, while other shades advance,
And other streaks of sunshine glance;
Thus checker'd is the life below
With gleams of joy, and clouds of wo,
Then hope not, while we journey on,
Still to be basking in the sun:
Nor fear, though now in shades ye mourn,
That sunshine will no more return.
If, by your terrors overcome,
Ye fly before th' approaching gloom,
The rapid clouds your flight pursue,
And darkness still o'ercasts your view.
Who longs to reach the radiant plain
Must onward urge his course amain;
For doubly swift the shadow flies,
When 'gainst the gale the pilgrim plies;
At least be firm, and undismay'd
Maintain your ground! the fleeting shade
Ere long spontaneous glides away,
And gives you back th' enlivening ray.
Lo, while I speak, our danger past!
No more the shrill horn's angry blast
Howls in our ear; the savage roar
Of war and murder is no more.
Then snatch the moment fate allows,

Nor think of past of future woes.'
He spoke; and hope revives; the lake
That instant one and all forsake,
In sweet amusement to employ
The present sprightly hour of joy.

Now from the western mountains brow
Compass'd with clouds of various glow,
The sun a broader orb displays,
And shoots aslope his ruddy rays.
The lawn assumes a fresher green,
And dew-drops spangle all the scene,
The balmy zephyr breathes along,
The shepherd sings his tender song,
With all their lays the groves resound,
And falling waters murmur round.
Discord and care were put to flight,
And all was peace, and calm delight.

The Wolf And Shepherds, A Fable
Laws, as we read in ancient sages,
Have been like cobwebs in all ages:
Cobwebs for little flies are spread,
And laws for little folks are made;
But if an insect of renown,
Hornet or beetle, wasp or drone,
Be caught in quest of sport or plunder,
The flimsy fetter flies in sunder.
Your simile perhaps may please one
With whom wit holds the place of reason:
But can you prove that this in fact is
Agreeable to life and practice?
Then hear, what in his simple way
Old Æsop told me t' other day.
In days of yore, but (which is very odd)
Our author mentions not the period,
We mortal men, less given to speeches,
Allow'd the beasts sometimes to teach us.
But now we all are prattlers grown,
And suffer no voice but our own;
With us no beast has leave to speak,
Although his honest heart should break.
'Tis true, your asses and your apes,
And other brutes in human shapes,
And that thing made of sound and show,
Which mortals have misnamed a beau,
(But in the language of the sky
Is call'd a two-legg'd butterfly),
Will make your very heartstrings ache

With loud and everlasting clack,
And beat your auditory drum,
Till you grow deaf, or they grow dumb.
But to our story we return:
'Twas early on a Summer morn,
A Wolf forsook the mountain den,
And issued hungry on the plain.
Full many a stream and lawn he past
And reach'd a winding vale at last;
Where from a hollow rock he spied
The shepherds drest in flowery pride.
Garlands were strew'd, and all was gay,
To celebrate a holiday.
The merry tabor's gamesome sound
Provoked the sprightly dance around.
Hard by a rural board was rear'd,
On which in fair array appear'd
The peach, the apple, and the raisin,
And all the fruitage of the season.
But, more distinguish'd than the rest,
Was seen a wether ready drest,
That smoking, recent from the flame,
Diffused a stomach-rousing steam.
Our Wolf could not endure the sight,
Courageous grew his appetite:
His entrails groan'd with tenfold pain,
He lick'd his lips, and lick'd again:
At last, with lightning in his eyes,
He bounces forth, and fiercely cries:
'Shepherds, I am not given to scolding,
But now my spleen I cannot hold in.
By Jove, such scandalous oppression
Would put an elephant in passion.
You, who your flocks (as you pretend)
By wholesome laws from harm defend,
Which make it death for any beast,
How much soe'er by hunger press'd,
To seize a sheep by force or stealth,
For sheep have right to life and health;
Can you commit, uncheck'd by shame,
What in a beast so much you blame?
What is a law, if those who make it
Become the forwardest to break it?
The case is plain: you would reserve
All to yourselves, while others starve.
Such laws from base self-interest spring,
Not from the reason of the thing—'
He was proceeding, when a swain
Burst out,—'And dares a wolf arraign
His betters, and condemn their measures,
And contradict their wills and pleasures?

We have establish'd laws, 'tis true,
But laws are made for such as you.
Know, sirrah, in its very nature
A law can't reach the legislature.
For laws, without a sanction join'd,
As all men know, can never bind;
But sanctions reach not us the makers,
For who dares punish us, though breakers?
'Tis therefore plain, beyond denial,
That laws were ne'er design'd to tie all;
But those, whom sanctions reach alone:
We stand accountable to none.
Besides, 'tis evident, that, seeing
Laws from the great derive their being,
They as in duty bound should love
The great, in whom they live and move,
And humbly yield to their desires:
'Tis just what gratitude requires.
What suckling, dandled on the lap,
Would tear away its mother's pap?
But hold—Why deign I to dispute
With such a scoundrel of a brute?
Logic is lost upon a knave,
Let action prove the law our slave.'
An angry nod his will declared
To his gruff yeoman of the guard;
The full-fed mongrels, train'd to ravage,
Fly to devour the shaggy savage.
The beast had now no time to lose
In chopping logic with his foes;
'This argument,' quoth he, 'has force,
And swiftness is my sole resource.'
He said, and left the swains their prey,
And to the mountains scour'd away.

Ode On Lord Hay's Birthday
A Muse, unskill'd in venal praise,
Unstain'd with flattery's art;
Who loves simplicity of lays
Breathed ardent from the heart;
While gratitude and joy inspire,
Resumes the long-unpractised lyre,
To hail, O H*, thy Natal Morn:
No gaudy wreathe of flowers she weaves,
But twines with oak the laurel leaves,
Thy cradle to adorn.

For not on beds of gaudy flowers
Thine ancestors reclined,

Where Sloth dissolves, and Spleen devours
All energy of mind.
To hurl the dart, to ride the car,
To stem the deluges of war,
And snatch from fate a sinking land:
Tremble th' Invader's lofty crest,
And from his grasp the dagger wrest,
And desolating brand:

'Twas this, that raised th' illustrious Line
To match the first in Fame!
A thousand years have seen it shine
With unabated flame.
Have seen thy mighty Sires appear
Foremost in Glory's high career,
The pride and pattern of the Brave.
Yet, pure from lust of blood their sire,
And from Ambition's wild desire,
They triumph'd but to save.

The Muse with joy attends their way,
The vale of Peace along;
There to its Lord the village gay
Renews the grateful song.
Yon castle's glittering towers contain
No pit of wo, nor clanking chain,
Nor to the suppliant's wail resound:
The open doors the needy bless,
Th' unfriended hail their calm recess,
And gladness smiles around.

There, to the sympathetic heart,
Life's best delights belong,
To mitigate the mourner's smart,
To guard the weak from wrong.
Ye Sons of Luxury, be wise:
Know, happiness for ever flies
The cold and solitary breast;
Then let the social instinct glow
And learn to feel another's wo,
And in his joy be bless'd.

O yet, ere Pleasure plant her snare
For unsuspecting youth;
Ere Flattery her song prepare
To check the voice of Truth;
O may his country's guardian Power
Attend the slumbering Infant's bower,
And bright, inspiring dreams impart;
To rouse th' hereditary fire,
To kindle each sublime desire,

Exalt, and warm the heart.

Swift to reward a Parent's fears,
A Parent's hopes to crown,
Roll on in peace, ye blooming years,
That rear him to renown;
When in his finish'd form and face
Admiring multitudes shall trace
Each patrimonial charm combined,
The courteous yet majestic mien,
The liberal smile, the look serene,
The great and gentle mind.

Yet, though thou draw a nation's eyes,
And win a nation's love,
Let not thy towering mind despise
The village and the grove.
No slander there shall wound thy fame,
No ruffian take his deadly aim.
No rival weave the secret snare;
For Innocence with angel smile
Simplicity that knows no guile,
And Love and Peace are there.

When winds the mountain oak assail,
And lay its glories waste,
Content may slumber in the vale,
Unconscious of the blast.
Through scenes of tumult while we roam,
The heart, alas! is ne'er at home,
It hopes in time to roam no more;
The mariner, not vainly brave,
Combats the storm, and rides the wave,
To rest at last on shore.

Ye proud, ye selfish, ye severe,
How vain your mask of state!
The good alone have joy sincere,
The good alone are great:
Great, when, amid the vale of peace,
They bid the plaint of sorrow cease,
And hear the voice of artless praise;
As when along the trophied plain
Sublime they lead the victor train,
While shouting nations gaze.

Law

Laws, as we read in ancient sages,
Have been like cobwebs in all ages.

Cobwebs for little flies are spread,
And laws for little folks are made;
But if an insect of renown,
Hornet or beetle, wasp or drone,
Be caught in quest of sport or plunder,
The flimsy fetter flies in sunder.

Epitaph (To This Grave Is Committed)

I was a friend, On this sad stone a pious look bestow,
Nor uninstructed read this tale of woe;
And while the sigh of sorrow heaves thy breast,
Let each rebellious murmur be supprest;
Heaven's hidden ways to trace, for us, how vain!
Heaven's wise decrees, how impious, to arraign!
Pure from the stains of a polluted age,
In early bloom of life, they left the stage:
Not doom'd in lingering woe to waste their breath
One moment snatch'd Them from the power of Death:
They liv'd united, and united died;
Happy the friends, whom Death cannot divi
O man, to thee, to all.

To The Right Honourable Lady Charlotte Gordon

Why, Lady, wilt thou bind thy lovely brow
With the dread semblance of that warlike helm,
That nodding plume, and wreathe of various glow,
That graced the chiefs of Scotia's ancient realm?

Thou know'st that virtue is of power the source,
And all her magic to thy eyes is given;
We own their empire, while we feel their force,
Beaming with the benignity of heaven.

The plumy helmet, and the martial mien,
Might dignify Minerva's awful charms;
But more resistless far th' Idalian queen -
Smiles, graces, gentleness, her only arms.

On The Report Of A Monument To Be Erected In Westminster Abbey, To The Memory Of A Late Author (Churchill)

Bufo, begone! with thee may Faction's fire,
That hatch'd thy salamander-fame, expire.
Fame, dirty idol of the brainless crowd,
What half-made moon-calf can mistake for good!
Since shared by knaves of high and low degree;

Cromwell and Cataline: Guido Faux, and thee.
By nature uninspired, untaught by art;
With not one thought that breathes the feeling heart,
With not one offering vow'd to Virtue's shrine,
With not one pure unprostituted line;
Alike debauch'd in body, soul, and lays;
For pension'd censure, and for pension'd praise,
For ribaldry, for libels, lewdness, lies,
For blasphemy of all the good and wise:
Coarse violence in coarser doggrel writ,
Which bawling blackguards spell'd, and took for wit:
For conscience, honour, slighted, spurn'd, o'erthrown:
Lo! Bufo shines the minion of renown.
Is this the land that boasts a Milton's fire,
And magic Spenser's wildly warbling lyre?
The land that owns the omnipotence of song,
When Shakspeare whirls the throbbing heart along?
The land, where Pope, with energy divine,
In one strong blaze bade wit and fancy shine:
Whose verse, by truth in virtue's triumph born,
Gave knaves to infamy, and fools to scorn;
Yet pure in manners, and in thought refined,
Whose life and lays adorn'd and bless'd mankind?
Is this the land, where Gray's unlabour'd art
Soothes, melts, alarms, and ravishes the heart:
While the lone wanderer's sweet complainings flow
In simple majesty of manly woe:
Or while, sublime, on eagle pinion driven,
He soars Pindaric heights, and sails the waste of Heaven?
Is this the land, o'er Shenstone's recent urn,
Where all the Loves and gentler Graces mourn?
And where, to crown the hoary bard of night,
The Muses and the Virtues all unite?
Is this the land where Akenside displays
The bold yet temperate flame of ancient days?
Like the rapt sage, in genius as in theme,
Whose hallow'd strain renown'd Illyssus' stream:
Or him, the indignant bard, whose patriot ire,
Sublime in vengeance, smote the dreadful lyre:
For truth, for liberty, for virtue warm,
Whose mighty song unnerved a tyrant's arm,
Hush'd the rude roar of discord, rage, and lust,
And spurn'd licentious demagogues to dust.
Is this the queen of realms? the glorious isle,
Britannia, blest in Heaven's indulgent smile?
Guardian of truth, and patroness of art,
Nurse of the undaunted soul, and generous heart!
Where, from a base unthankful world exiled,
Freedom exults to roam the careless wild:
Where taste to science every charm supplies,
And genius soars unbounded to the skies?

And shall a Bufo's most polluted name
Stain her bright tablet of untainted fame?
Shall his disgraceful name with theirs be join'd,
Who wish'd and wrought the welfare of their kind?
His name, accurst, who, leagued with — and Hell,
Labour'd to rouse, with rude and murderous yell,
Discord the fiend, to toss rebellion's brand,
To whelm in rage and woe a guiltless land:
To frustrate wisdom's, virtue's noblest plan,
And triumph in the miseries of man.
Drivelling and dull, when crawls the reptile Muse,
Swoln from the sty, and rankling from the stews,
With envy, spleen, and pestilence replete,
And gorged with dust she lick'd from Treason's feet:
Who once, like Satan, raised to Heaven her sight,
But turn'd abhorrent from the hated light:
O'er such a Muse shall wreaths of glory bloom?
No—shame and execration be her doom.
Hard-fated Bufo, could not dulness save
Thy soul from sin, from infamy thy grave?
Blackmore and Quarles, those blockheads of renown,
Lavish'd their ink, but never harm'd the town.
Though this, thy brother in discordant song,
Harass'd the ear, and cramp'd the labouring tongue:
And that, like thee, taught staggering prose to stand,
And limp on stilts of rhyme around the land.
Harmless they dozed a scribbling life away,
And yawning nations own'd the innoxious lay,
But from thy graceless, rude, and beastly brain,
What fury breathed the incendiary strain?
Did hate to vice exasperate thy style?
No—Bufo match'd the vilest of the vile.
Yet blazon'd was his verse with Virtue's name
Thus prudes look down to hide their want of shame:
Thus hypocrites to truth, and fools to sense,
And fops to taste, have sometimes made pretence:
Thus thieves and gamesters swear by honour's laws:
Thus pension-hunters bawl 'their country's cause:'
Thus furious Teague for moderation raved,
And own'd his soul to liberty enslaved.
Nor yet, though thousand cits admire thy rage,
Though less of fool than felon marks thy page:
Nor yet, though here and there one lonely spark
Of wit half brightens through the involving dark,
To show the gloom more hideous for the foil,
But not repay the drudging reader's toil;
(For who for one poor pearl of clouded ray
Through Alpine dunghills delves his desperate way?
Did genius to thy verse such bane impart?
No. 'Twas the demon of thy venom'd heart,
(Thy heart with rancour's quintessence endued).

And the blind zeal of a misjudging crowd.
Thus from rank soil a poison'd mushroom sprung,
Nursling obscene of mildew and of dung:
By Heaven design'd on its own native spot
Harmless to enlarge its bloated bulk, and rot.
But gluttony the abortive nuisance saw;
It roused his ravenous, undiscerning maw:
Gulp'd down the tasteless throat, the mess abhorr'd
Shot fiery influence round the maddening board.
O had thy verse been impotent as dull,
Nor spoke the rancorous heart, but lumpish scull;
Had mobs distinguish'd, they who howl'd thy fame,
The icicle from the pure diamond's flame,
From fancy's soul thy gross imbruted sense,
From dauntless truth thy shameless insolence,
From elegance confusion's monstrous mass,
And from the lion's spoils the skulking ass,
From rapture's strain the drawling doggrel line,
From warbling seraphim the grunting swine;
With gluttons, dunces, rakes, thy name had slept,
Nor o'er her sullied fame Britannia wept:
Nor had the Muse, with honest zeal possess'd,
To avenge her country, by thy name disgraced,
Raised this bold strain for virtue, truth, mankind,
And thy fell shade to infamy resign'd.
When frailty leads astray the soul sincere,
Let mercy shed the soft and manly tear.
When to the grave descends the sensual sot,
Unnamed, unnoticed, let his carrion rot.
When paltry rogues, by stealth, deceit, or force,
Hazard their necks, ambitious of your purse:
For such the hangman wreaths his trusty gin,
And let the gallows expiate their sin.
But when a ruffian, whose portentous crimes,
Like plagues and earthquakes terrify the times,
Triumphs through life, from legal judgment free,
For Hell may hatch what law could ne'er foresee:
Sacred from vengeance shall his memory rest?
Judas, though dead, though damn'd, we still detest.

Nature
O how canst thou renounce the boundless store
Of charms which Nature to her votary yields!
The warbling woodland, the resounding shore,
The pomp of groves, and garniture of fields;
All that the genial ray of morning gilds,
And all that echoes to the song of even,
All that the mountain's sheltering bosom shields,
And all the dread magnificence of heaven,

O how canst thou renounce and hope to be forgiven!

Life And Immortality

'O ye wild groves, oh, where is now your bloom!'
(The muse interprets thus his tender thought)
Your flowers, your verdure, and your balmy gloom,
Of late so grateful in the hour of drought?
Why do the birds, that song and rapture brought
To all your bowers, their mansions now forsake?
Ah! why has fickle chance this ruin wrought?
For now the storm howls mournful through the brake,
And the dead foliage flies in many a shapeless flake.

Where now the rill, melodious, pure, and cool,
And meads, with life, and mirth, and beauty crown'd?
Ah! see, the unsightly slime, and sluggish pool,
Have all the solitary vale embrown'd;
Fled each fair form, and mute each melting sound,
The raven croaks forlorn on naked spray:
And, hark: the river, bursting every mound,
Down the vale thunders, and with wasteful sway,
Uproots the grove, and rolls the shatter'd rocks away.

Yet such the destiny of all on earth:
So flourishes and fades majestic man.
Fair is the bud his vernal morn brings forth,
And fostering gales a while the nursling fan,
Oh, smile, ye heavens, serene; ye mildews wan,
Ye blighting whirlwinds, spare his balmy prime,
Nor lessen of his life the little span.
Borne on the swift, though silent wings of time,
Old age comes on apace to ravage all the clime.

And be it so. Let those deplore their doom
Whose hope still grovels in this dark sojourn;
But lofty souls, who look beyond the tomb,
Can smile at fate, and wonder how they mourn.
Shall spring to these sad scenes no more return?
Is yonder wave the sun's eternal bed?
Soon shall the orient with new lustre burn,
And spring shall soon her vital influence shed,
Again attune the grove, again adorn the mead.

'Shall I be left forgotten in the dust,
When fate, relenting, lets the flower revive?
Shall nature's voice, to man alone unjust,
Bid him, though doom'd to perish, hope to live?
Is it for this fair virtue oft must strive
With disappointment, penury, and pain?'

Nor heaven's immortal spring shall yet arrive,
And man's majestic beauty bloom again,
Bright through the eternal year of love's triumphant reign.

Pygmaeo-gerano-machia: The Battle Of The Pygmies and Cranes

From the Latin of Addison.

The pygmy-people, and the feather'd train,
Mingling in mortal combat on the plain,
I sing. Ye Muses, favour my designs,
Lead on my squadrons, and arrange the lines;
The flashing swords and fluttering wings display,
And long bills nibbling in the bloody fray;
Cranes darting with disdain on tiny foes,
Conflicting birds and men, and war's unnumber'd woes.

The wars and woes of heroes six feet long
Have oft resounded in Pierian song.
Who has not heard of Colcho's golden fleece,
And Argo mann'd with all the flower of Greece?
Of Thebes' fell brethren , Theseus stern of face,
And Peleus' son unrivall'd in the race,
Eneas founder of the Roman line,
And William glorious on the banks of Boyne?
Who has not learn'd to weep at Pompey's woes,
And over Blackmore's Epic page to doze?
'Tis I, who dare attempt unusual strains,
Of hosts unsung, and unfrequented plains;
The small shrill trump, and chiefs of little size,
And armies rushing down the darken'd skies.

Where India reddens to the early dawn,
Winds a deep vale from vulgar eyes withdrawn:
Bosom'd in groves the lowly region lies,
And rocky mountains round the border rise.
Here, till the doom of Fate its fall decreed,
The empire flourish'd of the pygmy-breed;
Here Industry perform'd, and Genius plann'd,
And busy multitudes o'erspread the land.
But now to these lone bounds if pilgrim stray,
Tempting through craggy cliffs the desperate way,
He finds the puny mansion fallen to earth,
Its godlings mouldering on th' abandon'd hearth;
And starts, where small white bones are spread around,
'Or little footsteps lightly print the ground;'
While the proud crane her nest securely builds,
Chattering amid the desolated fields.

But different fates befel her hostile rage,
While reign'd, invincible through many an age,
The dreaded Pygmy; roused by war's alarms
Forth rush'd the madding Mannikin to arms.
Fierce to the field of death the hero flies:
The faint crane fluttering flaps the ground, and dies;
And by the victor borne (o'erwhelming load!)
With bloody bill loose-dangling marks the road.
And oft the wily dwarf in ambush lay,
And often made the callow young his prey;
With slaughter'd victims heap'd his board, and smiled
T'avenge the parent's trespass on the child.
Oft where his feather'd foe had rear'd her nest,
And laid her eggs and household gods to rest,
Burning for blood, in terrible array,
The eighteen-inch militia burst their way;
All went to wreck; the infant foeman fell,
When scarce his chirping bill had broke the shell.

Loud uproar hence, and rage of arms arose,
And the fell rancour, of encountering foes;
Hence dwarfs and cranes one general havock whelms,
And Death's grim visage scares the pygmy-realms.
Not half so furious blazed the warlike fire
Of Mice, high theme of the Meonian lyre;
When bold to battle march'd th' accoutre'd frogs,
And the deep tumult thunder'd through the bogs.
Pierced by the javelin bulrush on the shore,
Here, agonizing, roll'd the mouse in gore;
And there the frog (a scene full sad to see!)
Shorn of one leg, slow sprawl'd along the three:
He vaults no more with vigorous hopes on high,
But mourns in hoarsest croaks his destiny.

And now the day of wo drew on apace,
A day of wo to all the pygmy race,
When dwarfs were doom'd (but penitence was vain)
To rue each broken egg and chicken slain.
For roused to vengeance by repeated wrong,
From distant climes the long-bill'd regions throng;
From Strymon's lake, Cayster's plashy meads,
And fens of Scythia green with rustling reeds;
From where the Danube winds through many a land,
And Mareotis laves th' Egyptian strand,
To rendezvous they waft on eager wing,
And wait assembled the returning spring.
Meanwhile they trim their plumes for length of flight,
Whet their keen beaks, and twisting claws, for fight;
Each crane the pygmy power in thought o'erturns,
And every bosom for the battle burns.

When genial gales the frozen air unbind,
The screaming legions wheel, and mount the wind.
Far in the sky they form their long array,
And land and ocean stretch'd immense survey
Deep deep beneath; and, triumphing in pride,
With clouds and winds commix'd, innumerous ride;
'Tis wild obstreperous clanguor all, and heaven
Whirls in tempestuous undulation driven.

Nor less th' alarm that shook the world below,
Where march'd in pomp of war th' embattled foe;
Where mannikins with haughty step advance,
And grasp the shield, and couch the quivering lance;
To right and left the lengthening lines they form,
And rank'd in deep array await the storm.

High in the midst the chieftain-dwarf was seen,
Of giant stature, and imperial mien.
Full twenty inches tall he strode along,
And view'd with lofty eye the wondering throng;
And, while with many a scar his visage frown'd,
Bared his broad bosom, rough with many a wound
Of beaks, and claws, disclosing to their sight
The glorious meed of high heroic might.
For with insatiate vengeance, he pursued,
And never ending hate, the feathery brood;
Unhappy they, confiding in the length
Of horny beak, or talon's crooked strength,
Who durst abide his rage; the blade descends,
And from the panting trunk the pinion rends.
Laid low in dust the pinion waves no more,
The trunk disfigured stiffens in its gore.
What hosts of heroes fell beneath his force!
What heaps of chicken carnage mark'd his course!
How oft, O Strymon, thy lone banks along,
Did wailing echo waft the funeral song.
And now from far the mingling clamours rise,
Loud and more loud rebounding through the skies.
From skirt to skirt of heaven, with stormy sway,
A cloud rolls on, and darkens all the day.
Near and more near descends the dreadful shade,
And now in battalions array display'd,
On sounding wings, and screaming in their ire,
The cranes rush onward, and the fight require.

The pygmy warrior's eye with fearless glare
The host thick swarming o'er the burthen'd air:
Thick swarming now, but to their native land
Doom'd to return a scanty straggling band.
When sudden, darting down the depth of heaven,
Fierce on th' expecting foe the cranes are driven.

The kindling phrenzy every bosom warms,
The region echoes to the crash of arms:
Loose feathers from the encountering armies fly,
And in careering whirlwinds mount the sky.
To breathe from toil upsprings the panting crane,
Then with fresh vigour downwards darts again.
Success in equal balance hovering hangs.
Here, on the sharp spear, mad with mortal pangs,
The bird transfix'd in bloody vortex whirls,
Yet fierce in death the threatening talon curls;
There, while the life-blood bubbles from his wound,
With little feet the pygmy beats the ground;
Deep from his breast the short short sob he draws,
And dying curses the keen pointed claws.
Trembles the thundering field thick cover'd o'er
With falchions, mangled wings, and streaming gore,
And Pygmy arms, and beaks of ample size,
And here a claw, and there a finger lies.

Encompass'd round with heaps of slaughter'd foes,
All grim in blood the pygmy champion glows,
And on th' assailing host impetuous springs,
Careless of nibbling bills, and flapping wings;
And midst the tumult whereso'er he turns,
The battle with redoubled fury burns;
From every side th' avenging cranes amain
Throng, to o'erwhelm this terror of the plain.
When suddenly (for such the will of Jove)
A fowl enormous, sousing from above,
The gallant chieftain clutch'd, and, soaring high,
(Sad chance of battle!) bore him p the sky.
The cranes pursue, and clustering in a ring,
Chatter triumphant round the captive king.
But ah! what pangs each pygmy bosom wrung,
When, now to cranes a prey on talons hung,
High in the clouds they saw their helpless lord,
His wriggling form still lessening as he soar'd.

Lo yet again with unabated rage
In mortal strife the mingling hosts engage.
The crane, with darted bill assaults the foe,
Hovering; then wheels aloft to scape the blow:
The dwarf in anguish aims the vengeful wound;
But whirls in empty air the falchion round.

Such was the scene, when midst the loud alarms
Sublime th' eternal Thunderer rose in arms.
When Briareus, by mad ambition driven,
Heaved Pelion huge, and hurl'd it high at heaven.
Jove roll'd redoubling thunders from on high,
Mountains and bolts encounter'd in the sky;

Till one stupendous ruin whelm'd the crew,
Their vast limbs weltering wide in brimstone blue.

But now at length the pygmy legions yield,
And wing'd with terror fly the fatal field.
They raise a weak and melancholy wail,
All in distraction scattering o'er the vale.
Prone on their routed rear the cranes descend;
Their bills bite furious, and their talons rend:
With unrelenting ire they urge the chase,
Sworn to exterminate the hated race.

'Twas thus the Pygmy Name, once great in war,
For spoils of conquer'd cranes renown'd afar,
Perish'd. For, by the dread decree of Heaven,
Short is the date earthly grandeur is given,
And vain are all attempts to roam beyond
Where Fate has fix'd the everlasting bound.
Fallen are the trophies of Assyrian power,
And Persia's proud dominion is no more;
Yea, though to both superior far in fame,
Thine empire, Latium, is an empty name.

And now with lofty chiefs of ancient time,
The pygmy heroes roam th' Elysian clime.
Or, if belief to matron-tales be due,
Full oft, in the belated shepherd's view,
Their frisking forms, in gentle green array'd,
Gambol secure amid the moonlight glade.
Secure, for no alarming cranes molest,
And all their woes in log oblivion rest;
Down the deep dale, and narrow winding way,
They foot it featly, ranged in ringlets gay:
'Tis joy and frolic all, where'er they rove,
And Fairy-people is the name they love.

Epitaph: Being Part Of An Inscription For A Monument
Farewell, my best-beloved; whose heavenly mind
Genius with virtue, strength with softness join'd;
Devotion, undebased by pride or art,
With meek simplicity, and joy of heart.
Though sprightly, gentle; though polite, sincere;
And only of thyself a judge severe;
Unblamed, unequall'd in each sphere of life,
The tenderest Daughter, Sister, Parent, Wife,
In thee, their Patroness, th' afflicted lost;
Thy friends, their pattern, ornament, and boast;
And I - but ah, can words my loss declare,
Or paint th' extremes of transport and despair!

O Thou, beyond what verse or speech can tell,
My guide, my friend, my best-beloved, farewell!

Epitaph On Two Young Men Of The Name Of Leitch,
Who Were Drowned In Crossing The River Southesk
O thou! whose steps in sacred reverence tread
These lone dominions of the silent dead;
On this sad stone a pious look bestow,
Nor uninstructed read this tale of woe;
And while the sigh of sorrow heaves thy breast,
Let each rebellious murmur be suppress'd;
Heaven's hidden ways to trace, for us how vain!
Heaven's wise decrees, how impious to arraign!
Pure from the stains of a polluted age,
In early bloom of life they left the stage:
Not doom'd in lingering woe to waste their breath,
One moment snatch'd them from the power of Death:
They lived united, and united died;
Happy the friends whom Death cannot divide!

Retirement
When in the crimson cloud of Even,
The lingering light decays,
And Hesper on the front of Heaven
His glittering gem displays!
Deep in the silent vale, unseen,
Beside a lulling stream,
A pensive Youth of placid mien,
Indulged this tender theme.

Ye cliffs, in hoary grandeur piled
High o'er the glimmering dale;
Ye woods, along whose windings wild
Murmurs the solemn gale;
Where Melancholy strays forlorn,
And Wo retires to weep,
What time the wan moon's yellow horn
Gleams on the western deep:

To you, ye wastes, whose artless charms
Ne'er drew Ambition's eye,
'Scaped a tumultuous world's alarms,
To your retreats I fly.
Deep in your most sequester'd bower
Let me at last recline,
Where Solitude, mild, modest Power,
Leans on her ivy'd shrine.

How shall I woo thee, matchless Fair!
Thy heavenly smile how win!
Thy smile, that smoothes the brow of Care,
And stills the storm within.
O wilt thou to thy favourite grove
Thine ardent votary bring,
And bless his hours, and bid them move
Serene, on silent wing.

Oft let remembrance soothe his mind
With dreams of former days,
When in the lap of Peace reclined
He framed his infant lays;
When Fancy roved at large, nor Care
Nor cold Distrust alarm'd,
Nor Envy with malignant glare
His simple youth had harm'd.

'Twas then, O Solitude, to thee
His early vows were paid,
From heart sincere, and warm, and free,
Devoted to the shade.
Ah why did Fate his steps decoy
In stormy paths to roam,
Remote from all congenial joy!
O take the wanderer home.

Thy shades, thy silence, now be mine,
Thy charms my only theme;
My haunt the hollow cliff, whose pine
Waves o'er the gloomy stream,
Whence the sacred owl on pinions gray
Breaks from the lone vale sails away
To more profound repose.

O while to thee the woodland pours
Its wildly-warbling song,
And balmy from the banks of flowers
The zephyr breathes along;
Let no rude sounds invade from far,
No vagrant foot be nigh,
No ray from Grandeur's gilded car,
Flash on the startled eye.

But if some pilgrim through the glade
Thy hallow'd bowers explore,
O guard from harm his hoary head,
And listen to his lore:
For he of joys divine shall tell
That wean from earthly wo,

And triumph o'er the mighty spell
That chains this heart below.

For me no more the path invites
Ambition loves to tread;
No more I climb those toilsome heights
By guileful Hope misled;
Leaps my fond fluttering heart no more
To mirth's enlivening strain;
For present pleasure soon is o'er,
And all the past is vain.

The Judgement Of Paris
Far in the depth of Ida's inmost grove,
A scene for love and solitude design'd;
Where flowery woodbines wild, by Nature wove,
Form'd the lone bower, the royal swain reclined.

All up the craggy cliffs, that tower'd to heaven,
Green waved the murmuring pines on every side;
Save where, fair opening to the beam of even,
A dale sloped gradual to the valley wide.

Echo'd the vale with many a cheerful note;
The lowing of the herds resounding long,
The shrilling pipe, and mellow horn remote,
And social clamours of the festive throng.

For now, low hovering o'er the western main,
Where amber clouds begirt his dazzling throne,
The Sun with ruddier verdure deck'd the plain;
And lakes and streams and spires triumphal shone.

And many a band of ardent youths were seen;
Some into rapture fired by glory's charms,
Or hurl'd the thundering car along the green,
Or march'd embattled on in glittering arms.

Others more mild, in happy leisure gay,
The darkening forest's lonely gloom explore,
Or by Scamander's flowery margin stray,
Or the blue Hellespont's resounding shore.

But chief the eye to Ilion's glories turn'd,
That gleam'd along the extended champaign far,
And bulwarks in terrific pomp adorn'd,
Where Peace sat smiling at the frowns of War.

Rich in the spoils of many a subject clime,

In pride luxurious blazed the imperial dome;
Tower'd 'mid the encircling grove the fane sublime,
And dread memorials mark'd the hero's tomb

Who from the black and bloody cavern led
The savage stern, and soothed his boisterous breast;
Who spoke, and Science rear'd her radiant head,
And brighten'd o'er the long benighted waste:

Or, greatly daring in his country's cause,
Whose heaven-taught soul the awful plan design'd,
Whence Power stood trembling at the voice of laws;
Whence soar'd on Freedom's wing the ethereal mind.

But not the pomp that royalty displays,
Nor all the imperial pride of lofty Troy,
Nor Virtue's triumph of immortal praise
Could rouse the langour of the lingering boy.

Abandon'd all to soft Enone's charms,
He to oblivion doom'd the listless day;
Inglorious lull'd in Love's dissolving arms,
While flutes lascivious breathed the enfeebling lay.

To trim the ringlets of his scented hair:
To aim, insidious, Love's bewitching glance;
Or cull fresh garlands for the gaudy fair,
Or wanton loose in the voluptuous dance:

These were his arts; these won Enone's love,
Nor sought his fetter'd soul a nobler aim.
Ah, why should beauty's smile those arts approve
Which taint with infamy the lover's flame?

Now laid at large beside a murmuring spring,
Melting he listen'd to the vernal song,
And Echo, listening, waved her airy wing,
While the deep winding dales the lays prolong;

When, slowly floating down the azure skies,
A crimson cloud flash'd on his startled sight,
Whose skirts gay-sparkling with unnumber'd dyes
Launch'd the long billowy trails of flickery light.

That instant, hush'd was all the vocal grove,
Hush'd was the gale, and every ruder sound;
And strains aërial, warbling far above,
Rung in the ear a magic peal profound.

Near and more near the swimming radiance roll'd;
Along the mountains stream the lingering fires;

Sublime the groves of Ida blaze with gold,
And all the Heaven resounds with louder lyres.

The trumpet breathed a note: and all in air,
The glories vanish'd from the dazzled eye;
And three ethereal forms, divinely fair,
Down the steep glade were seen advancing nigh.

The flowering glade fell level where they moved;
O'erarching high the clustering roses hung;
And gales from heaven on balmy pinion roved,
And hill and dale with gratulation rung.

The FIRST with slow and stately step drew near,
Fix'd was her lofty eye, erect her mien:
Sublime in grace, in majesty severe,
She look'd and moved a goddess and a queen.

Her robe along the gale profusely stream'd,
Light lean'd the sceptre on her bending arm;
And round her brow a starry circlet gleam'd,
Heightening the pride of each commanding charm.

Milder the NEXT came on with artless grace,
And on a javelin's quivering length reclined:
To exalt her mien she bade no splendour blaze,
Nor pomp of vesture fluctuate on the wind.

Serene, though awful, on her brow the light
Of heavenly wisdom shone; nor roved her eyes.
Save to the shadowy cliffs majestic height,
Or the blue concave of the involving skies.

Keen were her eyes to search the inmost soul:
Yet virtue triumph'd in their beams benign,
And impious Pride oft felt their dread control,
When in fierce lightning flash'd the wrath divine1.

With awe and wonder gazed the adoring swain;
His kindling cheeks great Virtue's power confess'd;
But soon 'twas o'er; for Virtue prompts in vain,
When Pleasure's influence numbs the nerveless breast.

And now advanced the QUEEN of melting JOY,
Smiling supreme in unresisted charms:
Ah, then, what transports fired the trembling boy!
How throbb'd his sickening frame with fierce alarms!

Her eyes in liquid light luxurious swim,
And languish with unutterable love.
Heaven's warm bloom glows along each brightening limb,

Where fluttering bland the veil's thin mantlings rove.

Quick, blushing as abash'd, she half withdrew:
One hand a bough of flowering myrtle waved.
One graceful spread, where, scarce conceal'd from view,
Soft through the parting robe her bosom heaved.

'Offspring of Jove supreme! beloved of Heaven!
Attend.' Thus spoke the Empress of the Skies.
'For know, to thee, high-fated prince, 'tis given
Through the bright realms of Fame sublime to rise,

Beyond man's boldest hope; if nor the wiles
Of Pallas triumph o'er the ennobling thought;
Nor Pleasure lure with artificial smiles
To quaff the poison of her luscious draught.

When Juno's charms the prize of beauty claim,
Shall aught on earth, shall aught in heaven contend?
Whom Juno calls to high triumphant fame,
Shall he to meaner sway inglorious bend?

Yet lingering comfortless in lonesome wild,
Where Echo sleeps 'mid cavern'd vales profound,
The pride of Troy, Dominion's darling child,
Pines while the slow hour stalks in sullen round.

Hear thou, of Heaven unconscious! From the blaze
Of glory, stream'd from Jove's eternal throne,
Thy soul, O mortal, caught the inspiring rays
That to a god exalt Earth's raptured son.

Hence the bold wish, on boundless pinion borne,
That fires, alarms, impels the maddening soul;
The hero's eye, hence, kindling into scorn,
Blasts the proud menace, and defies control.

But, unimproved, Heaven's noblest boons are vain,
No sun with plenty crowns the uncultured vale:
Where green lakes languish on the silent plain,
Death rides the billows of the western gale.

Deep in yon mountain's womb, where the dark cave
Howls to the torrent's everlasting roar,
Does the rich gem its flashy radiance wave?
Or flames with steady ray the imperial ore?

Toil deck'd with glittering domes yon champaign wide,
And wakes yon grove-embosom'd lawns to joy,
And rends the rough ore from the mountain's side,
Spangling with starry pomp the thrones of Troy.

Fly these soft scenes. Even now, with playful art,
Love wreathes the flowery ways with fatal snare;
And nurse the ethereal fire that warms thy heart,
That fire ethereal lives but by thy care.

Lo! hovering near on dark and dampy wing,
Sloth with stern patience waits the hour assign'd,
From her chill plume the deadly dews to fling,
That quench Heaven's beam, and freeze the cheerless mind.

Vain, then, the enlivening sound of Fame's alarms,
For Hope's exulting impulse prompts no more:
Vain even the joys that lure to Pleasure's arms,
The throb of transport is forever o'er.

O who shall then to Fancy's darkening eyes
Recall the Elysian dreams of joy and light?
Dim through the gloom the formless visions rise,
Snatch'd instantaneous down the gulf of night.

Thou who, securely lull'd in youth's warm ray,
Mark'st not the desolations wrought by Time,
Be roused or perish. Ardent for its prey,
Speeds the fell hour that ravages thy prime.

And, 'midst the horrors shrined of midnight storm,
The fiend Oblivion eyes thee from afar,
Black with intolerable frowns her form,
Beckoning the embattled whirlwinds into war.

Fanes, bulwarks, mountains, worlds, their tempest whelms;
Yet glory braves unmoved the impetuous sweep.
Fly then, ere, hurl'd from life's delightful realms,
Thou sink to Oblivion's dark and boundless deep.

Fly, then, where Glory points the path sublime,
See her crown dazzling with eternal light!
'Tis Juno prompts thy daring steps to climb,
And girds thy bounding heart with matchless might.

Warm in the raptures of divine desire,
Burst the soft chain that curbs the aspiring mind;
And fly where Victory, borne on wings of fire,
Waves her red banner to the rattling wind.

Ascend the car: indulge the pride of arms,
Where clarions roll their kindling strains on high,
Where the eye maddens to the dread alarms,
And the long shout tumultuous rends the sky.

Plunged in the uproar of the thundering field,
I see thy lofty arm the tempest guide:
Fate scatters lightning from thy meteor-shield,
And Ruin spreads around the sanguine tide.

Go, urge the terrors of thy headlong car
On prostrate Pride, and Grandeur's spoils o'erthrown,
While all amazed even heroes shrink afar,
And hosts embattled vanish at thy frown.

When glory crowns thy godlike toils, and all
The triumph's lengthening pomp exalts thy soul,
When lowly at thy feet the mighty fall,
And tyrants tremble at thy stern control:

When conquering millions hail thy sovereign might,
And tribes unknown dread acclamation join;
How wilt thou spurn the forms of low delight!
For all the ecstasies of heaven are thine:

For thine the joys, that fear no length of days,
Whose wide effulgence scorns all mortal bound:
Fame's trump in thunder shall announce thy praise,
Nor bursting worlds her clarion's blast confound.'

The Goddess ceased, not dubious of the prize:
Elate she mark'd his wild and rolling eye,
Mark'd his lip quiver, and his bosom rise,
And his warm cheek suffused with crimson dye.

But Pallas now drew near. Sublime, serene,
In conscious dignity she view'd the swain:
Then, love and pity softening all her mien,
Thus breathed with accents mild the solemn strain:

'Let those whose arts to fatal paths betray,
The soul with passion's gloom tempestuous blind,
And snatch from Reason's ken the auspicious ray
Truth darts from heaven to guide the exploring mind.

'But Wisdom loves the calm and serious hour,
When heaven's pure emanation beams confess'd:
Rage, ecstasy, alike disclaim her power,
She woo's each gentler impulse of the breast.

Sincere the unalter'd bliss her charms impart,
Sedate the enlivening ardours they inspire:
She bids no transient rapture thrill the heart,
She wakes no feverish gust of fierce desire.

Unwise, who, tossing on the watery way,

All to the storm the unfetter'd sail devolve:
Man more unwise resigns the mental sway,
Borne headlong on by passion's keen resolve.

While storms remote but murmur on thine ear,
Nor waves in ruinous uproar round thee roll,
Yet, yet a moment check thy prone career,
And curb the keen resolve that prompts thy soul.

Explore thy heart, that, roused by Glory's name,
Pants all enraptured with the mighty charm
And does Ambition quench each milder flame?
And is it conquest that alone can warm?

To indulge fell Rapine's desolating lust,
To drench the balmy lawn in streaming gore,
To spurn the hero's cold and silent dust
Are these thy joys? Nor throbs thy heart for more?

Pleased canst thou listen to the patriot's groan,
And the wild wail of Innocence forlorn?
And hear the abandon'd maid's last frantic moan,
Her love for ever from her bosom torn?

Nor wilt thou shrink, when Virtue's fainting breath
Pours the dread curse of vengeance on thy head?
Nor when the pale ghost bursts the cave of death,
To glare distraction on thy midnight bed?

Was it for this, though born to regal power,
Kind Heaven to thee did nobler gifts consign,
Bade Fancy's influence gild thy natal hour,
And bade Philanthropy's applause be thine?

Theirs be the dreadful glory to destroy,
And theirs the pride of pomp, and praise suborn'd,
Whose eye ne'er lighten'd at the smile of Joy,
Whose cheek the tear of Pity ne'er adorn'd:

Whose soul, each finer sense instinctive quell'd,
The lyre's mellifluous ravishment defies:
Nor marks where Beauty roves the flowery field,
Or Grandeur's pinion sweeps the unbounded skies.

Hail to sweet Fancy's unexpressive charm!
Hail to the pure delights of social love!
Hail, pleasures mild, that fire not while ye warm,
Nor rack the exulting frame, but gently move!

But Fancy soothes no more, if stern remorse
With iron grasp the tortured bosom wring.

Ah then! even Fancy speeds the venom's course,
Even Fancy points with rage the maddening sting.

Her wrath a thousand gnashing fiends attend,
And roll the snakes, and toss the brands of hell;
The beam of Beauty blasts: dark heavens impend
Tottering: and Music thrills with startling yell.

What then avails, that with exhaustless store
Obsequious Luxury loads thy glittering shrine?
What then avails, that prostrate slaves adore,
And Fame proclaims thee matchless and divine?

What though bland Flattery all her arts apply?
Will these avail to calm the infuriate brain?
Or will the roaring surge, when heaved on high,
Headlong hang, hush'd, to hear the piping swain?

In health how fair, how ghastly in decay
Man's lofty form! how heavenly fair the mind
Sublimed by Virtue's sweet enlivening sway!
But ah! to guilt's outrageous rule resign'd.

How hideous and forlorn! when ruthless Care
With cankering tooth corrodes the seeds of life,
And deaf with passion's storms when pines Despair,
And howling furies rouse the eternal strife.

Oh, by thy hopes of joy that restless glow,
Pledges of Heaven! be taught by Wisdom's lore;
With anxious haste each doubtful path forego,
And life's wild ways with cautious fear explore.

Straight be thy course: nor tempt the maze that leads
Where fell Remorse his shapeless strength conceals,
And oft Ambition's dizzy cliff he treads,
And slumbers oft in Pleasure's flowery vales.

Nor linger unresolved: Heaven prompts the choice,
Save when Presumption shuts the ear of Pride:
With grateful awe attend to Nature's voice,
The voice of Nature Heaven ordain'd thy guide.

Warn'd by her voice the arduous path pursue,
That leads to Virtue's fane a hardy band:
What though no gaudy scenes decoy their view,
Nor clouds of fragrance roll along the land?

What though rude mountains heave the flinty way?
Yet there the soul drinks light and life divine,
And pure aërial gales of gladness play,

Brace every nerve, and every sense refine.

Go, prince, be virtuous and be blest. The throne
Rears not its state to swell the couch of Lust:
Nor dignify Corruption's daring son,
To o'erwhelm his humbler brethren of the dust.

But yield an ampler scene to Bounty's eye,
An ampler range to Mercy's ear expand:
And, 'midst admiring nations, set on high
Virtue's fair model, framed by Wisdom's hand.

Go then: the moan of Woe demands thine aid:
Pride's licensed outrage claims thy slumbering ire:
Pale Genius roams the bleak neglected shade,
And battening Avarice mocks his tuneless lyre.

Even Nature pines, by vilest chains oppress'd:
The astonish'd kingdoms crouch to Fashion's nod.
O ye pure inmates of the gentle breast,
Truth, Freedom, Love, O where is your abode?

O yet once more shall Peace from heaven return,
And young Simplicity with mortals dwell!
Nor Innocence the august pavilion scorn,
Nor meek Contentment fly the humble cell!

Wilt thou, my prince, the beauteous train implore
'Midst earth's forsaken scenes once more to bide?
Then shall the shepherd sing in every bower,
And Love with garlands wreathe the domes of Pride.

The bright tear starting in the impassion'd eyes
Of silent Gratitude: the smiling gaze
Of Gratulation, faltering while he tries
With voice of transport to proclaim thy praise:

The ethereal glow that stimulates thy frame,
When all the according powers harmonious move,
And wake to energy each social aim,
Attuned spontaneous to the will of Jove:

Be these, O man, the triumphs of thy soul;
And all the conqueror's dazzling glories slight,
That meteor-like o'er trembling nations roll,
To sink at once in deep and dreadful night.

Like thine, yon orb's stupendous glories burn
With genial beam; nor, at the approach of even,
In shades of horror leave the world to mourn,
But gild with lingering light the empurpled heaven.'

Thus while she spoke, her eye, sedately meek,
Look'd the pure fervour of maternal love.
No rival zeal intemperate flush'd her cheek
Can Beauty's boast the soul of Wisdom move?

Worth's noble pride, can Envy's leer appal,
Or staring Folly's vain applauses soothe?
Can jealous Fear Truth's dauntless heart enthrall?
Suspicion lurks not in the heart of Truth.

And now the shepherd raised his pensive head:
Yet unresolved and fearful roved his eyes,
Scared at the glances of the awful maid;
For young unpractised Guilt distrusts the guise

Of shameless Arrogance.—His wavering breast,
Though warm'd by Wisdom, own'd no constant fire,
While lawless Fancy roam'd afar, unblest
Save in the oblivious lap of soft Desire.

When thus the queen of soul-dissolving smiles:
'Let gentler fate my darling prince attend,
Joyless and cruel are the warrior's spoils,
Dreary the path stern Virtue's sons ascend.

Of human joy full short is the career,
And the dread verge still gains upon your sight;
While idly gazing far beyond your sphere,
Ye scan the dream of unapproach'd delight:

Till every sprightly hour and blooming scene
Of life's gay morn unheeded glides away,
And clouds of tempests mount the blue serene,
And storms and ruin close the troublous day.

Then still exult to hail the present joy,
Thine be the boon that comes unearn'd by toil;
No forward vain desire thy bliss annoy,
No flattering hope thy longing hours beguile.

Ah! why should man pursue the charms of Fame,
For ever luring, yet for ever coy?
Light as the gaudy rainbow's pillar'd gleam,
That melts illusive from the wondering boy!

What though her throne irradiate many a clime,
If hung loose-tottering o'er the unfathom'd tomb?
What though her mighty clarion, rear'd sublime,
Display the imperial wreath and glittering plume?

Can glittering plume, or can the imperial wreath
Redeem from unrelenting fate the brave?
What note of triumph can her clarion breathe,
To alarm the eternal midnight of the grave?

That night draws on: nor will the vacant hour
Of expectation linger as it flies:
Nor fate one moment unenjoy'd restore:
Each moment's flight how precious to the wise!

O shun the annoyance of the bustling throng,
That haunt with zealous turbulence the great:
There coward Office boasts the unpunish'd wrong,
And sneaks secure in insolence of state.

O'er fancied injury Suspicion pines,
And in grim silence gnaws the festering wound:
Deceit the rage-embitter'd smile refines,
And Censure spreads the viperous hiss around.

Hope not, fond prince, though Wisdom guard thy throne,
Though Truth and Bounty prompt each generous aim,
Though thine the palm of peace, the victor's crown,
The Muse's rapture, and the patriot's flame:

Hope not, though all that captivates the wise,
All that endears the good exalt thy praise:
Hope not to taste repose: for Envy's eyes
At fairest worth still point their deadly rays.

Envy, stern tyrant of the flinty heart,
Can aught of Virtue, Truth, or Beauty charm?
Can soft Compassion thrill with pleasing smart,
Repentance melt, or Gratitude disarm?

Ah no. Where Winter Scythia's waste enchains,
And monstrous shapes roar to the ruthless storm,
Not Phoebus' smile can cheer the dreadful plains,
Or soil accursed with balmy life inform.

Then, Envy, then is thy triumphant hour,
When mourns Benevolence his baffled scheme:
When Insult mocks the clemency of Power,
And loud dissension's livid firebrands gleam:

When squint-eyed Slander plies the unhallow'd tongue,
From poison'd maw when Treason weaves his line,
And Muse apostate (infamy to song!)
Grovels, low muttering, at Sedition's shrine.

Let not my prince forego the peaceful shade,

The whispering grove, the fountain and the plain:
Power, with the oppressive weight of pomp array'd,
Pants for simplicity and ease in vain.

The yell of frantic Mirth may stun his ear,
But frantic Mirth soon leaves the heart forlorn;
And Pleasure flies that high tempestuous sphere:
Far different scenes her lucid paths adorn.

She loves to wander on the untrodden lawn,
Or the green bosom of reclining hill,
Soothed by the careless warbler of the dawn,
Or the lone plaint of ever-murmuring rill.

Or from the mountain glade's aërial brow,
While to her song a thousand echoes call,
Marks the wide woodland wave remote below,
Where shepherds pipe unseen, and waters fall.

Her influence oft the festive hamlet proves,
Where the high carol cheers the exulting ring;
And oft she roams the maze of wildering groves,
Listening the unnumber'd melodies of Spring.

Or to the long and lonely shore retires;
What time, loose-glimmering to the lunar beam,
Faint heaves the slumberous wave, and starry fires
Gild the blue deep with many a lengthening gleam.

Then to the balmy bower of Rapture borne,
While strings self-warbling breathe Elysian rest,
Melts in delicious vision, till the morn
Spangle with twinkling dew the flowery waste.

The frolic Moments, purple-pinion'd, dance
Around, and scatter roses as they play;
And the blithe Graces, hand in hand, advance,
Where, with her loved compeers, she deigns to stray;

Mild Solitude, in veil of rustic dye,
Her sylvan spear with moss-grown ivy bound;
And Indolence, with sweetly languid eye,
And zoneless robe that trails along the ground;

But chiefly Love—O thou, whose gentle mind
Each soft indulgence Nature framed to share;
Pomp, wealth, renown, dominion, all resign'd,
Oh, haste to Pleasure's bower, for Love is there.

Love, the desire of Gods! the feast of heaven!
Yet to Earth's favour'd offspring not denied!

Ah! let not thankless man the blessing given
Enslave to Fame, or sacrifice to Pride.

Nor I from Virtue's call decoy thine ear;
Friendly to Pleasure are her sacred laws:
Let Temperance' smile the cup of gladness cheer;
That cup is death, if he withhold applause.

Far from thy haunt be Envy's baneful sway,
And Hate, that works the harass'd soul to storm;
But woo Content to breathe her soothing lay,
And charm from Fancy's view each angry form.

No savage joy the harmonious hours profane!
Whom Love refines, can barbarous tumults please?
Shall rage of blood pollute the sylvan reign?
Shall Leisure wanton in the spoils of Peace?

Free let the feathery race indulge the song,
Inhale the liberal beam, and melt in love:
Free let the fleet hind bound her hills along,
And in pure streams the watery nations rove.

To joy in Nature's universal smile
Well suits, O man, thy pleasurable sphere;
But why should Virtue doom thy years to toil?
Ah! why should Virtue's laws be deem'd severe?

What meed, Beneficence, thy care repays?
What, Sympathy, thy still returning pang?
And why his generous arm should Justice raise,
To dare the vengeance of a tyrant's fang?

From thankless spite no bounty can secure;
Or froward wish of discontent fulfil,
That knows not to regret thy bounded power,
But blames with keen reproach thy partial will.

To check the impetuous all-involving tide
Of human woes, how impotent thy strife!
High o'er thy mounds devouring surges ride,
Nor reck thy baffled toils, or lavish'd life.

The bower of bliss, the smile of love be thine,
Unlabour'd ease, and leisure's careless dream.
Such be their joys who bend at Venus' shrine,
And own her charms beyond compare supreme.'

Warm'd as she spoke, all panting with delight,
Her kindling beauties breathed triumphant bloom;
And Cupids flutter'd round in circlets bright,

And Flora pour'd from all her stores perfume.

'Thine be the prize,' exclaim'd the enraptured youth,
'Queen of unrivall'd charms, and matchless joy.'
O blind to fate, felicity, and truth!
But such are they whom Pleasure's snares decoy.

The Sun was sunk; the vision was no more;
Night downward rush'd tempestuous, at the frown
Of Jove's awaken'd wrath: deep thunders roar,
And forests howl afar, and mountains groan,

And sanguine meteors glare athwart the plain;
With horror's scream the Ilian towers resound,
Raves the hoarse storm along the bellowing main,
And the strong earthquake rends the shuddering ground.

The Triumph Of Melancholy

Memory, be still! why throng upon the thought
These scenes deep-stain'd with Sorrow's sable dye?
Hast thou in store no joy-illumined draught,
To cheer bewilder'd Fancy's tearful eye?

Yes—from afar a landscape seems to rise,
Deck'd gorgeous by the lavish hand of Spring:
Thin gilded clouds float light along the skies,
And laughing Loves disport on fluttering wing.

How blest the youth in yonder valley laid!
Soft smiles in every conscious feature play,
While to the gale low murmuring through the glade,
He tempers sweet his sprightly-warbling lay.

Hail, Innocence! whose bosom, all serene,
Feels not fierce Passion's raving tempest roll!
Oh, ne'er may Care distract that placid mien!
Oh, ne'er may Doubt's dark shades o'erwhelm thy soul!

Vain wish! for, lo! in gay attire conceal'd,
Yonder she comes, the heart-inflaming fiend!
(Will no kind power the helpless stripling shield?)
Swift to her destined prey see Passion bend!

O smile accursed, to hide the worst designs!
Now with blithe eye she woo's him to be blest,
While round her arm unseen a serpent twines
And, lo! she hurls it hissing at his breast.

And, instant, lo! his dizzy eyeball swims

Ghastly, and reddening darts a threatful glare;
Pain with strong grasp distorts his writhing limbs,
And Fear's cold hand erects his bristling hair!

Is this, O life, is this thy boasted prime?
And does thy spring no happier prospect yield?
Why gilds the vernal sun thy gaudy clime,
When nipping mildews waste the flowery field?

How Memory pains! Let some gay theme beguile
The musing mind, and soothe to soft delight.
Ye images of woe, no more recoil;
Be life's past scenes wrapt in oblivious night.

Now when fierce Winter, arm'd with wasteful power,
Heaves the wild deep that thunders from afar,
How sweet to sit in this sequester'd bower,
To hear, and but to hear, the mingling war!

Ambition here displays no gilded toy
That tempts on desperate wing the soul to rise,
Nor Pleasure's flower-embroider'd paths decoy,
Nor Anguish lurks in Grandeur's gay disguise.

Oft has Contentment cheer'd this lone abode
With the mild languish of her smiling eye;
Here Health has oft in blushing beauty glow'd,
While loose-robed Quiet stood enamour'd by.

Even the storm lulls to more profound repose:
The storm these humble walls assails in vain:
Screen'd is the lily when the whirlwind blows,
While the oak's stately ruin strews the plain.

Blow on, ye winds! Thine, Winter, be the skies;
Roll the old ocean, and the vales lay waste:
Nature thy momentary rage defies;
To her relief the gentler seasons haste.

Throned in her emerald car, see Spring appear!
(As Fancy wills, the landscape starts to view)
Her emerald car the youthful Zephyrs bear,
Fanning her bosom with their pinions blue.

Around the jocund Hours are fluttering seen;
And, lo! her rod the rose-lipp'd power extends.
And, lo! the lawns are deck'd in living green,
And Beauty's bright-eyed train from heaven descends.

Haste, happy days, and make all nature glad
But will all nature joy at your return?

Say, can ye cheer pale Sickness' gloomy bed,
Or dry the tears that bathe the untimely urn?

Will ye one transient ray of gladness dart
'Cross the dark cell where hopeless slavery lies?
To ease tired Disappointment's bleeding heart,
Will all your stores of softening balm suffice?

When fell Oppression in his harpy fangs
From Want's weak grasp the last sad morsel bears,
Can ye allay the heart-wrung parent's pangs,
Whose famish'd child craves help with fruitless tears?

For ah! thy reign, Oppression, is not past,
Who from the shivering limbs the vestment rends,
Who lays the once rejoicing village waste,
Bursting the ties of lovers and of friends.

O ye, to Pleasure who resign the day,
As loose in Luxury's clasping arms you lie,
O yet let pity in your breast bear sway,
And learn to melt at Misery's moving cry.

But hop'st thou, Muse, vain-glorious as thou art,
With the weak impulse of thy humble strain,
Hop'st thou to soften Pride's obdurate heart,
When Errol's bright example shines in vain?

Then cease the theme. Turn, Fancy, turn thine eye,
Thy weeping eye, nor further urge thy flight;
Thy haunts, alas! no gleams of joy supply,
Or transient gleams, that flash and sink in night.

Yet fain the mind its anguish would forego
Spread then, historic Muse, thy pictured scroll;
Bid thy great scenes in all their splendour glow,
And swell to thought sublime the exalted soul.

What mingling pomps rush boundless on the gaze!
What gallant navies ride the heaving deep!
What glittering towns their cloud-wrapt turrets raise!
What bulwarks frown horrific o'er the steep!

Bristling with spears, and bright with burnish'd shields,
The embattled legions stretch their long array;
Discord's red torch, as fierce she scours the fields,
With bloody tincture stains the face of day.

And now the hosts in silence wait the sign.
How keen their looks whom Liberty inspires!
Quick as the Goddess darts along the line,

Each breast impatient burns with noble fires.

Her form how graceful! In her lofty mien
The smiles of Love stern Wisdom's frown control;
Her fearless eye, determined though serene,
Speaks the great purpose, and the unconquer'd soul.

Mark, where Ambition leads the adverse band,
Each feature fierce and haggard, as with pain!
With menace loud he cries, while from his hand
He vainly strives to wipe the crimson stain.

Lo! at his call, impetuous as the storms,
Headlong to deeds of death the hosts are driven:
Hatred to madness wrought, each face deforms,
Mounts the black whirlwind, and involves the heaven.

Now, Virtue, now thy powerful succour lend,
Shield them for Liberty who dare to die
Ah, Liberty! will none thy cause befriend?
Are these thy sons, thy generous sons, that fly?

Not Virtue's self, when Heaven its aid denies,
Can brace the loosen'd nerves or warm the heart!
Not Virtue's self can still the burst of sighs,
When festers in the soul Misfortune's dart.

See where, by heaven-bred terror all dismay'd
The scattering legions pour along the plain;
Ambition's car, with bloody spoils array'd,
Hews its broad way, as Vengeance guides the rein.

But who is he that, by yon lonely brook,
With woods o'erhung and precipices rude,
Abandon'd lies, and with undaunted look
Sees streaming from his breast the purple flood?

Ah, Brutus! ever thine be Virtue's tear!
Lo! his dim eyes to Liberty he turns,
As scarce supported on her broken spear
O'er her expiring son the goddess mourns.

Loose to the wind her azure mantle flies,
From her dishevell'd locks she rends the plume;
No lustre lightens in her weeping eyes,
And on her tear-stain'd cheek no roses bloom.

Meanwhile the world, Ambition, owns thy sway,
Fame's loudest trumpet labours in thy praise,
For thee the Muse awakes her sweetest lay,
And Flattery bids for thee her altars blaze.

Nor in life's lofty bustling sphere alone,
The sphere where monarchs and where heroes toil,
Sink Virtue's sons beneath Misfortune's frown,
While Guilt's thrill'd bosom leaps at Pleasure's smile;

Full oft, where Solitude and Silence dwell,
Far, far remote, amid the lowly plain,
Resounds the voice of Woe from Virtue's cell:
Such is man's doom, and Pity weeps in vain.

Still grief recoils—How vainly have I strove
Thy power, O Melancholy, to withstand!
Tired I submit; but yet, O yet remove
Or ease the pressure of thy heavy hand.

Yet for a while let the bewilder'd soul
Find in society relief from woe;
O yield a while to Friendship's soft control;
Some respite, Friendship, wilt thou not bestow?

Come, then, Philander! for thy lofty mind
Looks down from far on all that charms the great;
For thou canst bear, unshaken and resign'd,
The brightest smiles, the blackest frowns of Fate:

Come thou, whose love unlimited, sincere,
Nor faction cools, nor injury destroys;
Who lend'st to misery's moans a pitying ear,
And feel'st with ecstasy another's joys:

Who know'st man's frailty: with a favouring eye,
And melting heart, behold'st a brother's fall;
Who, unenslaved by custom's narrow tie,
With manly freedom follow'st reason's call.

And bring thy Delia, softly-smiling fair,
Whose spotless soul no sordid thoughts deform:
Her accents mild would still each throbbing care,
And harmonize the thunder of the storm.

Though blest with wisdom, and with wit refined,
She courts not homage, nor desires to shine:
In her each sentiment sublime is join'd
To female sweetness, and a form divine.

Come, and dispel the deep surrounding shade:
Let chasten'd mirth the social hours employ;
O catch the swift-wing'd hour before 'tis fled,
On swiftest pinion flies the hour of joy.

Even while the careless disencumber'd soul
Dissolving sinks to joy's oblivious dream,
Even then to time's tremendous verge we roll
With haste impetuous down life's surgy stream.

Can Gaiety the vanish'd years restore,
Or on the withering limbs fresh beauty shed,
Or soothe the sad inevitable hour,
Or cheer the dark, dark mansions of the dead?

Still sounds the solemn knell in Fancy's ear,
That call'd Cleora to the silent tomb;
To her how jocund roll'd the sprightly year!
How shone the nymph in beauty's brightest bloom!

Ah! beauty's bloom avails not in the grave,
Youth's lofty mien, nor age's awful grace:
Moulder unknown the monarch and the slave,
Whelm'd in the enormous wreck of human race.

The thought-fix'd portraiture, the breathing bust,
The arch with proud memorials array'd,
The long-lived pyramid shall sink in dust
To dumb oblivion's ever-desert shade.

Fancy from comfort wanders still astray.
Ah, Melancholy! how I feel thy power!
Long have I labour'd to elude thy sway!
But 'tis enough, for I resist no more.

The traveller thus, that o'er the midnight waste
Through many a lonesome path is doom'd to roam,
Wilder'd and weary sits him down at last;
For long the night, and distant far his home.

The Minstrel; Or, The Progress Of Genius : Book I.

I.
Ah! who can tell how hard it is to climb
The steep where Fame's proud temple shines afar!
Ah! who can tell how many a soul sublime
Hath felt the influence of malignant star,
And wag'd with Fortune an eternal war!
Check'd by the scoff of Pride, by Envy's frown,
And Poverty's unconquerable bar,
In life's low vale remote hath pin'd alone
Then dropt into the grave, unpitied and unknown!

II.

And yet, the languor of inglorious days
Not equally oppressive is to all.
Him, who ne'er listen'd to the voice of praise,
The silence of neglect can ne'er appal.
There are, who, deaf to mad Ambition's call,
Would shrink to hear th' obstreperous trump of Fame;
Supremely blest, if to their portion fall
Health, competence, and peace. Nor higher aim
Had he, whose simple tale these artless lines proclaim.

III.

This sapient age disclaims all classic lore;
Else I should here in cunning phrase display,
How forth The Minstrel far'd in days of yore,
Right glad of heart, though homely in array;
His waving locks and beard all hoary grey:
And, from his bending shoulder, decent hung
His harp, the sole companion of his way,
Which to the whistling wind responsive rung:
And ever as he went some merry lay he sung.

IV.

Fret not yourselves, ye silken sons of pride,
That a poor Wanderer should inspire my strain.
The Muses Fortune's fickle smile deride,
Nor ever bow the knee in Mammon's fane;
For their delights are with the village-train,
Whom Nature's laws engage, and Nature's charms:
They hate the sensual, and scorn the vain;
The parasite their influence never warms,
Nor him whose sordid soul the love of wealth alarms.

V.

Though richest hues the peacock's plumes adorn,
Yet horror screams from his discordant throat.
Rise, sons of harmony, and hail the morn,
While warbling larks on russet pinions float;
Or seek at noon the woodland scene remote,
Where the grey linnets carol from the hill.
O let them ne'er with artificial note,
To please a tyrant, strain the little bill,
But sing what Heaven inspires, and wander where they will.

VI.

Liberal, not lavish, is kind Nature's hand;
Nor was perfection made for man below.
Yet all her schemes with nicest art are plann'd,
Good counteracting ill, and gladness woe.
With gold and gems if Chilian mountains glow,
If bleak and barren Scotia's hills arise;
There plague and poison, lust and rapine grow;

Here peaceful are the vales, and pure the skies,
And freedom fires the soul, and sparkles in the eyes.

VII.
Then grieve not, thou to whom th' indulgent Muse
Vouchsafes a portion of celestial fire;
Nor blame the partial Fates, if they refuse
Th' imperial banquet, and the rich attire.
Know thine own worth, and reverence the lyre.
Wilt thou debase the heart which God refin'd?
No; let thy heaven-taught soul to heaven aspire,
To fancy, freedom, harmony, resign'd;
Ambition's groveling crew for ever left behind.

VIII.
Canst thou forego the pure ethereal soul,
In each fine sense so exquisitely keen,
On the dull couch of Luxury to loll,
Stung with disease and stupified with spleen;
Fain to implore the aid of Flattery's screen,
Even from thyself thy loathsome heart to hide
(The mansion then no more of joys serene)
Where fear, distrust, malevolence, abide,
And impotent desire, and disappointed pride?

IX.
O how canst thou renounce the boundless store
Of charms which Nature to her votary yields!
The warbling woodland, the resounding shore,
The pomp of groves, and garniture of fields;
All that the genial ray of morning gilds,
And all that echoes to the song of even,
All that the mountain's sheltering bosom shields,
And all that dread magnificence of heaven,
O how canst thou renounce, and hope to be forgiven!

X.
These charms shall work thy soul's eternal health,
And love, and gentleness, and joy, impart.
But these thou must renounce, if lust or wealth
E'er win its way to thy corrupted heart;
For, ah! it poisons like a scorpion's dart,
Prompting th' ungenerous wish, the selfish scheme,
The stern resolve, unmoved by pity a smart,
The troublous day, and long distressful dream -
Return my roving Muse, resume thy purposed theme.

XI.
There lived in Gothic days, as legends tell,
A shepherd-swain, a man of low degree;
Whose sires, perchance, in Fairyland might dwell,

Sicilian groves, or vales of Arcady;
But he, I ween, was of the north country:
A nation famed for song, and beauty's charms;
Zealous, yet modest; innocent, though free;
Patient of toil; serene amidst alarms;
Inflexible in faith; invincible in arms.

XII.
The shepherd-swain of whom I mention made,
On Scotia's mountains fed his little flock;
The sickle, sithe, or plough, he never sway'd:
An honest heart was almost all his stock;
His drink the living water from the rock:
The milky dams supplied his board, and lent
Their kindly fleece to baffle winter's shock:
And he, though oft with dust and sweat besprent,
Did guide and guard their wanderings, wheresoe'er they went.

XIII.
From labour health, from health contentment springs,
Contentment opes the source of every joy.
He envied not, he never thought of kings;
Nor form those appetites sustain'd annoy,
That chance may frustrate, or indulgence cloy:
Nor fate his calm and humble hopes beguiled;
He morn'd no recreant friend, nor mistress coy,
For on his vows the blameless Phoebe smiled,
And her alone he loved, and loved her from a child.

XIV.
No jealousy their dawn of love o'ercast,
Nor blasted were their wedded days with strife;
Each season look'd delightful, as it pass'd,
To the fond husband, and the faithful wife.
Beyond the lowly vale of shepherd life
They never roam'd; secure beneath the storm
Which in ambition's lofty land is rife,
Where peace and love are canker'd by the worm
Of pride, each bud of joy industrious to deform.

XV.
The wight, whose tales these artless lines unfold,
Was all the offspring of this humble pair.
His birth no oracle or seer foretold:
No prodigy appear'd in death or air,
Nor aught that might a strange event declare.
You guess each circumstance of Edwin's birth;
The parent's transport, and the parent's care;
The gossip's prayer for wealth, and wit, and worth:
And one long summer-day of indolence and mirth.

XVI.

And yet poor Edwin was no vulgar boy;
Deep thought oft seem'd to fix his infant eye.
Dainties he heeded not, nor gaude, nor toy,
Save one short pipe of rudest minstrelsy.
Silent when glad; affectionate, though shy;
And now his look was most demurely sad,
And now he laugh'd aloud, yet none knew why.
The neighbours stared and sigh'd, yet bless'd the lad;
Some deem'd him wonderous wise, and some believed him mad.

XVII.

But why should I his childish feats display?
Concourse, and noise, and toil, he ever fled;
Nor cared to mingle in the clamorous fray
Of squabbling imps, but to the forest sped,
Or roam'd at large the lonely mountain's head;
Or, where the maze of some bewilder'd stream
To deep untrodden groves his footsteps led,
There would he wander wild, 'till Phoebus' beam,
Shot from the western cliff, released the weary team.

XVIII.

Th' exploit of strength, dexterity, or speed,
To him nor vanity nor joy could bring.
His heart, from cruel sport estranged, would bleed
To work the wo of any living thing,
By trap, or net; by arrow, or by sling;
These he detested, those he scorn'd to wield:
He wish'd to be the guardian, not the king.
Tyrant far less, or traitor of the field.
And sure the sylvan reign unbloody joy might yield.

XIX.

Lo! where the stripling, wrapp'd in wonder, roves
Beneath the precipice o'er hung with pine;
And sees, on high, amidst th' encircling groves,
From cliff to cliff the foaming torrents shine:
While waters, woods, and winds, in concert join,
And Echo swells the chorus to the skies.
Would Edwin this majestic scene resign
For aught the huntsman's puny craft supplies?
Ah! no: he better knows great Nature's charms to prize.

XX.

And oft he traced the uplands, to survey,
When o'er the sky advanced the kindling dawn,
The crimson cloud, blue main, and mountain gray,
And lake, dim gleaming on the smoky lawn;
Far to the west the long, long vale withdrawn,
Where twilight loves to linger for a while;

And now he faintly kens the bounding fawn,
And villager abroad at early toil. -
But, lo! the sun appears! and heaven, earth, ocean, smile.

XXI.
And oft the craggy cliff he loved to climb,
When all in mist the world below was lost.
What dreadful pleasure! there to stand sublime,
Like shipwreck'd mariners on desert coast,
And view th' enormous waste of vapour, toss'd
In billows, lengthening to th' horizon round
Now scoop'd in gulphs, with mountains now emboss'd!
And hear the voice of mirth and song rebound,
Flocks, herds, and waterfalls, along the hoar profound.

XXII.
In truth he was a strange and wayward wight,
Fond of each gentle, and each dreadful scene.
In darkness, and in storm, he found delight:
Nor less, than when on ocean wave serene
The southern sun diffused his dazzling sheen.
Even sad vicissitude amused his soul:
And if a sigh would sometimes intervene,
And down his cheek a tear of pity roll,
A sigh, a tear, so sweet, he wish'd not to control.

XXIII.
'O ye wild groves, O where is now your bloom!'
(The Muse interprets thus his tender thought).
'Your flowers, your verdure, and your balmy gloom,
Of late so grateful in the hour of drought!
Why do the birds, that song and rapture brought
To all your bowers, their mansions now forsake?
Ah! why has fickle chance this ruin wrought?
For now the storm howls mournful thro' the brake,
And the dead foliage flies in many a shapeless flake.

XXIV.
'Where now the rill, melodious, pure, and cool,
And meads, with Life, and mirth, and beauty crown'd!
Ah! see, th' unsightly slime, and sluggish pool,
Have all the solitary vale imbrown'd;
Fled each fair form, and mute each melting sound,
The raven croaks forlorn on naked spray:
And, hark! the river, bursting every mound,
Down the vale thunders; and, with wasteful sway,
Uproots the grove, and rolls the shatter'd rocks away.

XXV.
'Yet such the destiny of all on earth;
So flourishes and fades majestic man.

Fair is the bud his vernal morn brings forth,
And fostering gales a while the nursling fan.
O smile, ye heavens, serene; ye mildews wan,
Ye blighting whirlwinds, spare his balmy prime,
Nor lessen of his life the little span.
Borne on the swift, though silent, wings of Time,
Old age comes on apace to ravage all the clime.

XXVI.
'And be it so. Let those deplore their doom,
Whose hope still grovels in the dark sojourn.
But lofty souls, who look beyond the tomb,
Can smile at Fate, and wonder how they mourn.
Shall spring to these sad scenes no more return?
Is yonder wave the sun's eternal bed?
Soon shall the orient with new lustre burn,
And spring shall soon her vital influence shed,
Again attune the grove, again adorn the mead.

XXVII.
'Shall I be left abandon'd in the dust,
When Fate, relenting, let's the flower revive?
Shall Nature's voice, to man alone unjust,
Bid him, though doom'd to perish, hope to live?
Is it for this fair virtue oft must strive
With disappointment, penury, and pain?
No: Heaven's immortal spring shall yet arrive;
And man's majestic beauty bloom again,
Bright through th' eternal year of Love's triumphant reign.'

XXVIII.
This truth, sublime his simple sire had taught,
In sooth, 'twas almost all the shepherd knew.
No subtle nor superfluous lore he sought,
Nor ever wish'd his Edwin to pursue.
'Let man's own sphere (quoth he) confine his view,
Be man's peculiar work his sole delight.'
And much, and oft, he warn'd him to eschew
Falsehood and guile, and aye maintain the right,
By pleasure unseduced, unawed by lawless might.

XXIX.
'And, from the prayer of Want, and plaint of Wo,
O never, never turn away thine ear.
Forlorn in this bleak wilderness below,
Ah! what were man, should heaven refuse to hear!
To others do (the law is not severe)
What to thyself thou wishest to be done.
Forgive thy foes; and love thy parent's dear,
And friends, and native land; nor those alone;
All human weal and wo learn thou to make thine own.'

XXX.

See in the rear of the warm sunny shower,
The visionary boy from shelter fly!
For now the storm of summer-rain is o'er,
And cool, and fresh, and fragrant, is the sky!
And, lo! in the dark east, expanded high,
The rainbow brightens to the setting sun:
Fond fool, that deem'st the streaming glory nigh,
How vain the chase thine ardour has begun!
'Tis fled afar, ere half thy purposed race be run.

XXXI.

Yet couldst thou learn, that thus it fares with age,
When pleasure, wealth, or power, the bosom warm,
This baffled hope might tame thy manhood's rage,
And disappointment of her sting disarm. -
But why should foresight thy fond heart alarm?
Perish the lore that deadens young desire!
Pursue, poor imp, th' imaginary charm,
Indulge gay Hope, and Fancy's pleasing fire:
Fancy and Hope too soon shall of themselves expire.

XXXII.

When the long-sounding curfew from afar
Loaded with loud lament the lonely gale,
Young Edwin, lighted by the evening star,
Lingering and listening wander'd down the vale.
There would he dream of graves, and corses pale;
And ghosts, that to the charnel-dungeon throng,
And drag a length of clanking chain, and wail,
Till silenced by the owl's terrific song,
Or blast that shrieks by fits the shuddering aisles along.

XXXIII.

Or when the setting moon, in crimon died,
Hung o'er the dark and melancholy deep,
To haunted stream, remote from man he hied,
Where Fays of yore their revels wont to keep;
And there let Fancy roam at large, till sleep
A vision brought to his entraced sight.
And first, a wildly-murmuring wind 'gan creep
Shrill to his ringing ear; then tapers bright,
With instantaneous gleam, illumed the vault of Night.

XXXIV.

Anon in view a portal's blazon'd arch
Arose; the trumpet bids the valves unfold;
And forth a host of little warriors march,
Grasping the diamond lance, and targe of gold.
Their look was gentle, their demeanour bold,

And green their healms, and green their silk attire.
And here and there, right venerably old,
The long-robed minstrels wake the warbling wire,
And some with mellow breath the martial pipe inspire.

XXXV.

With merriment, and song, and timbrels clear,
A troop of dames from myrtle bowers advance:
The little warriors doff the targe and spear,
And loud enlivening strains provoke the dance.
They meet, they dart away, they wheek askance
To right, to left, they thrid the flying maze;
Now bound aloft with vigorous spring, then glance
Rapid along: with many-colour'd rays
Of tapers, gems, and gold, and echoing forests blaze.

XXXVI.

The dream is fled. Proud harbinger of day,
Who scar'dst the vision with thy clarion shrill,
Fell chanticleer! who oft has reft away
My fancied good, and brought substantial ill!
O to thy cursed scream, discordant still,
Let Harmony aye shut her gentle ear:
Thy boastful mirth let jealous rivals spill,
Insult thy crest, and glossy pinions tear,
And ever in thy dream the ruthless fox appear!

XXXVII.

Forbear, my Muse. Let Love attune thy line.
Revoke the spell. Thine Edwin frets not so.
For how should he at wicked chance repine,
Who feels from every change amusement flow?
Even now his eyes with smiles of rapture glow,
As on he wanders through the scenes of morn,
Where the fresh flowers in living lustre blow,
Where thousand pearls the dewy lawns adorn,
A thousand notes of joy in every breeze are borne.

XXXVIII

But who the melodies of morn can tell?
The wild brook babbling down the mountain-side;
The lowing herd; the sheepfold's simple bell;
The pipe of early shepherd dim descried
In the lone valley; echoing far and wide
The clamorous horn along the cliffs above;
The hollow murmur of the ocean-tide;
The hum of bees, and linnet's lay of love,
And the full choir that wakes the universal grove.

XXXIX

The cottage-curs at early pilgrim bark;

Crown'd with her pail the tripping milkmaid sings;
The whistling plowman stalks afield; and, hark!
Down the rough slope the ponderous waggon rings;
Through rustling corn the hare astonish'd springs;
Slow tolls the village-clock the drowsy hour;
The partridge bursts away on whirring wings;
Deep mourns the turtle in sequester'd bower,
And shrill lark carols clear from her aereal tower.

XL.
O Nature, how in every charm supreme!
Whose votaries feast on raptures ever new!
O for the voice and fire of seraphim,
To sing thy glories with devotion due!
Blest be the day I scap'd the wrangling crew,
From Pyrrho's maze, and Epicurus' sty;
And held high converse with the godlike few,
Who to th' enraptur'd heart, and ear, and eye,
Teach beauty, virtue, truth, and love, and melody.

XLI.
Hence! ye, who snare and stupefy the mind,
Sophists, of beauty, virtue, joy, the bane!
Greedy and fell, though impotent and blind,
Who spread your filthy nets in Truth's fair fane,
And ever ply your venom'd fangs amain!
Hence to dark Error's den, whose rankling slime
First gave you form! hence! lest the Muse should deign,
(Though loth on theme so mean to waste a rhyme),
With vengeance to pursue your sacrilegious crime.

XLII.
But hail, ye mighty masters of the lay,
Nature's true sons, the friends of man and truth!
Whose song, sublimely sweet, serenely gay,
Amus'd my childhood, and inform'd my youth.
O let your spirit still my bosom soothe,
Inspire my dreams, and my wild wanderings guide.
Your voice each rugged path of life can smooth;
For well I know, wherever ye reside,
There harmony, and peace, and innocence, abide.

XLIII.
Ah me! abandon'd on the lonesome plain,
As yet poor Edwin never knew your lore,
Save when against the winter's drenching rain,
And driving snow, the cottage shut the door.
Then as instructed by tradition hoar,
Her legend when the Beldam 'gan impart,
Or chant the old heroic ditty o'er,
Wonder and joy ran thrilling to his heart;

Much he the tale admired, but more the tuneful art.

XLIV.
Various and strange was the long-winded tale;
And halls, and knights, and feats of arms, display'd;
Or merry swains, who quaff the nut-brown ale,
And sing, enamour'd of the nut-brown maid;
The moonlight revel of the fairy glade;
Or hags, that suckle the infernal brood,
And ply in caves th' unutterable trade,
'Midst fiends and spectres, quench the moon in blood,
Yell in the midnight storm, or ride th' infuriate flood.

XLV.
But when to horror his amazement rose,
A gentler strain the Beldam would rehearse,
A tale of rural life, a tale of woes,
The orphan-babes, and guardian uncle fierce.
O cruel! will no pang of pity pierce
That heart by lust of lucre sear'd to stone!
For sure, if aught of virtue last, or verse,
To latest times shall tender soul bemoan
Those helpless orphan-babes by thy fell arts undone.

XLVI.
Behold, with berries smear'd, with brambles torn,
The babes now famish'd lay them down to die,
'Midst the wild howl of darksome woods forlorn,
Folded in one another's arms they lie;
Nor friend, nor stranger, hears their dying cry:
'For from the town the man returns no more.'
But thou, who Heaven's just vengeance dar'st defy
This deed with fruitless tears shalt soon deplore,
When Death lays waste thy house, and flames consume thy store.

XLVII.
A stifled of stern vindictive joy
Brighten'd one moment Edwin's starting tear. -
'But why should gold man's feeble mind decoy,
And innocence thus die by doom severe?'
O Edwin! while thy heart is yet sincere,
Th' assaults of discontent and doubt repel:
Dark even at noontide is our mortal sphere;
But let us hope, - to doubt, is to rebel,
Let us exult in hope, that all shall yet be well.

XLVIII.
Nor be thy generous indignation check'd,
Nor check'd the tender tear to Misery given;
From Guilt's contagious power shall that protect,
This soften and refine the soul for Heaven.

But dreadful is their doom, whom doubt has driven
To censure Fate, and pious Hope forego:
Like yonder blasted boughs by lightning riven,
Perfection, beauty, life, they never know,
But frown on all that pass, a monument of wo.

XLIX.
Shall he, whose birth, maturity, and age,
Scarce fill the circle of one summer day,
Shall the poor gnat with discontent and rage
Exclaim, that Nature hastens to decay,
If but a cloud obstruct the solar ray,
If but a momentary shower descend!
Or shall frail man Heaven's dread decree gainsay
Which bade the series of events extend
Wide through unnumber'd worlds, and wages without end!

L.
One part, one little part, we dimly scan
Thro' the dark medium of life's feverish dream;
Yet dare arraign the whole stupendous plan,
If but that little part incongruous seem.
Nor is that part perhaps what mortals deem;
Oft from apparent ill our blessings rise.
O then renounce that impious self-esteem,
That alms to trace the secrets of the skies:
For thou art but of dust; be humble, and be wise.

LI.
Thus Heaven enlarged his soul in riper years
For Nature gave him strength and fire, to soar
On Fancy's wing above this vale of tears;
Where dark, cold-hearted sceptics, creeping, pore
Through microscope of metaphysic lore:
And much they grope for truth, but never hit.
For why? their powers, inadequate before,
This art preposterous renders more unfit;
Yet deem they darkness light, and their vain blunders wit.

LII.
Nor was this ancient dame a foe to mirth.
Her ballad, jest, and riddle's quaint device
Oft cheer'd the shepherds round their social hearth,
Whom levity or spleen could ne'er entice
To purchase chat or laughter, at the price
Of decency. Nor let it faith exceed,
That Nature forms a rustic taste so nice.
Ah! had they been of court or city breed,
Such delicacy were right marvellous indeed.

LIII.

Oft when winter-storm had ceased to rave,
He roam'd the snowy waste at even, to view
The cloud stupendous, from th' Atlantic wave
High-towering, sail along th' horizon blue:
Where 'midst the changeful scenery ever new
Fancy a thousand wondrous forms descries
More wildly great than ever pencil drew,
Rocks, torrents, gulfs, and shapes of giant size,
And glittering cliffs on cliffs, and fiery ramparts rise.

LIV.
Thence musing onward to the sounding shore,
The lone enthusiast oft would take his way,
Listening with pleasing dread to the deep roar
Of the wide-weltering waves. In black array
When sulphurous clouds roll'd on the vernal day,
Even then he hasten'd from the haunt of man,
Along the trembling wilderness to stray,
What time the lightnings fierce career began,
And o'er heaven's rending arch the rattling thunder ran.

LV.
Responsive to the sprightly pipe when all
In sprightly dance the village-youth were join'd,
Edwin of melody aye held in thrall,
From the rude gambol far remote reclined,
Soothed with the soft notes warbling in the wind.
Ah then, all jollity seem'd noise and folly,
To the pure soul by Fancy's fire refined,
Ah, what is mirth but turbulence unholy,
When with the charm compared of heavenly melancholy!

LVI.
Is there a heart that music cannot melt?
Alas! how is that rugged heart forlorn!
Is there, who ne'er those mystic transports felt
Of solitude and melancholy born?
He needs not woo the Muse; he is her scorn.
The sophist's rope of cobweb he shall twine;
Mope o'er the schoolman's peevish page; or mourn,
And delve for life in Mammon's dirty mine;
Sneak with the scoundrel fox, or grunt with glutton swine.

LVII.
For Edwin Fate a nobler doom had plann'd;
Song was his favourite and first pursuit.
The wild harp rang to his breath the plaintive hand,
And languish'd to his breath the plaintive flute.
His infant muse, though artless, was not mute:
Of elegance as yet he took no care;
For this of time and culture is the fruit;

And Edwin gain'd at last this fruit so rare:
As in some future verse I suppose to declare.

LVIII.
Meanwhile, whate'er of beautiful, or new,
Sublime, or dreadful, in earth, sea, or sky,
By chance, or search, was offer'd to his view;
He scann'd with curious and romantic eye.
Whate'er of lore tradition could supply
From Gothic tale, or song, or fable old,
Roused him, still keen to listen and to pry.
At last, though long by penury controll'd,
And solitude, his soul her graces 'gan unfold.

LIX.
Thus on the chill Lapponian's dreary land,
For many a long month lost in snow profound,
When Sol from Cancer sends the season bland,
And in their northern cave the storms are bound;
From silent mountains, straight, with starting sound
Torrents are hurl'd; green hills emerge; and lo,
The trees with foliage, cliffs with flowers are crown'd;
Pure rills through vales of verdure warbling go:
And wonder, love, and joy, the peasant's heart o'erflow.

LX.
Here pause, my Gothic lyre, a little while,
The leisure hour is all that thou canst claim;
But on this verse of Montague should smile,
New strains ere long shall animate thy frame:
And her applause to me is more than fame;
For still with truth accords her taste refined.
At lucre or renown let others aim,
I only wish to please the gentle mind,
Whom Nature's charms inspire, and love of human kind.

The Minstrel; Or, The Progress Of Genius : BookL II.
I.
Of chance or change O let not man complain,
Else shall he never never cease to wail:
For, from the imperial dome, to where the swain
Rears the lone cottage in the silent dale,
All feel the assault of fortune's fickle gale;
Art, empire, earth itself to change are doom'd;
Earthquakes have raised to heaven the humble vale,
And gulphs the mountain's mighty mass entomb'd,
And where the Atlantic rolls wide continents have bloom'd.

II.

But sure to foreign climes we need not range,
Nor search the ancient records of our race,
To learn the dire effects of time and change,
Which in ourselves, alas! we daily trace.
Yet at the darken'd eye, the wither'd face,
Or hoary hair, I never will repine:
But spare, O Time, whate'er of mental grace,
Of candour, love, or sympathy divine,
Whate'er of fancy's ray, of friendship's flame is mine.

III.
So I, obsequious to Truth's dread command,
Shall here without reluctance change my lay,
And smile to the Gothic lyre with harsher hand;
Now when I leave that flowery path for aye
Of childhood, where I sported many a day,
Warbling and sauntering carelessly along;
Where every face was innocent and gay,
Each vale romantic, tuneful every tongue,
Sweet, wild, and artless all, as Edwin's infant song.

IV.
'Perish the lore that deadens young desire,'
Is the soft tenor of my song no more.
Edwin, though loved of Heaven, must not aspire
To bliss, which mortals never knew before.
On trembling wings let youthful fancy soar,
Nor always haunt the sunny realms of joy;
But now and then the shades of life explore;
Though many a sound and sight of wo annoy,
And many a qualm of care his rising hopes destroy.

V.
Vigour from toil, from trouble patience grows.
The weakly bosom, warm in summer bower,
Some tints of transient beauty may disclose;
But soon it withers in the chilling hour.
Mark yonder oak. Superior to the power
Of all the warring winds of heaven they rise,
And from the stormy promontory tower,
And toss their giant arms amid the skies,
While each assailing blast increase the strength supplies.

VI.
And now the downy cheek and deepen'd voice
Gave dignity to Edwin's blooming prime;
And walks of wider circuit were his choice,
And vales more wild, and mountains more sublime.
One evening, as he framed the careless rhyme,
It was his chance to wander far abroad,
And o'er a lonely eminence to climb,

Which heretofore his foot had never trode;
A vale appear'd below, a deep retired abode.

VII.
Thither he hied enamour'd of the scene:
For rocks on rocks piled, as by magic spell,
Here scorch'd with lightning, there with ivy green,
Fenced from the north and east this savage del;
Southward a mountain rose with easy swell,
Whose long long groves eternal murmur made,
And toward the western sun a streamlet fell,
Where, through the cliffs, the eye, remote, survey'd
Blue hills, and glittering waves, and skies in gold array'd.

VIII.
Along this narrow valley you might see
The wild deer sporting on the meadow ground,
And, here and there, a solitary tree,
Or mossy stone, or rock with woodbine crown'd.
Oft did the cliffs reverberate the sound
Of parted fragments tumbling from on high;
And from the summit of that craggy mound
The perching eagle oft was heard to cry,
Or on resounding wings to shoot athwart the sky.

IX.
One cultivated spot there was, that spread
Its flowery bosom to the noonday beam,
Where many a rose-bud rears its blushing head,
And herbs for food with future plenty teem.
Sooth'd by the lulling sound of grove and stream
Romantic visions swarm on Edwin's soul:
He minded not the sun's last trembling gleam,
Nor heard from afar the twilight curfew toll; -
When slowly on his ear these moving accents stole.

X.
'Hail, awful scenes, that calm the troubled breast,
And woo the weary to profound repose;
Can passion's wildest uproar lay to rest,
And whisper comfort to the man of woes!
Here Innocence may wander, safe from foes,
And Contemplation soar on seraph wings.
O Solitude, the man who thee forgoes,
When lucre lures him, or ambition stings,
Shall never know the source whence real grandeur springs.

XI.
'Vain man, is grandeur given to gay attire?
Then let the butterfly thy pride upbraid: -
To friends, attendant, armies, bought with hire?

It is thy weakness that requires their aid, -
To palaces, with gold and gems inlay'd?
They fear the thief, and tremble in the storm; -
To hosts, through carnage who to conquests wade?
Behold the victor vanquish'd by the worm!
Behold, what deeds of wo the locust can perform!

XII.
'True dignity is his, whose tranquil mind
Virtue has raised above the things below,
Who, every hope and fear to heaven resign'd,
Shrinks not, though Fortune aim her deadliest blow.'
- This strain from 'midst the rocks was heard to flow
In solemn sounds. Now beam'd the evening star,
And from embattled clouds emerging slow,
Cynthia came riding on her silver car;
And hoary mountain-cliffs shone faintly from afar.

XIII.
Soon did the solemn voice its theme renew;
(While Edwin wrapp'd in wonder listening stood)
'Ye tools and toys of tyranny, adieu,
Scorn'd by the wise, and hated by the good!
Ye only can engage the service brood
Of Levity and Lust, who all their days,
Ashamed of truth and liberty, have woo'd,
And hugg'd the chain, that glittering on their gaze
Seems to outshine the pomp of heaven's empyreal blaze.

XIV.
'Like them, abandon'd to ambition's sway,
I sought for glory in the paths of guile;
And fawn'd and smiled to plunder and betray,
Myself betray'd and plunder'd all the while;
So gnaw'd the viper the corroding file.
But now with pangs of keen remorse I rue
Those years of trouble and debasement vile
Yet why should I this cruel theme pursue!
Fly, fly, detested thoughts, for ever from my view.

XV.
'The gusts of appetite, the clouds of care,
And storms of disappointment, all o'erpass'd,
Henceforth no earthly hope with heaven shall share
This heart where peace serenely shines at last.
And if for me no treasure be amass'd,
And if no future age shall hear my name,
I lurk the more secure from fortune's blast,
And with more leisure feed this pious flame,
Whose rapture far transcends the fairest hopes of fame.

XVI.
'The end and the reward of toil is rest.
Be all my prayer for virtue and for peace.
Of wealth and fame, of pomp and power possess'd,
Who ever felt his weight of wo decrease!
Ah! what avails the lore of Rome and Greece,
The lay heaven-prompted, and harmonious
The dust of Ophir, or the Tyrian fleece,
All that art, fortune, enterprise, can bring,
If envy, scorn, remorse, or pride the bosom wring?

XVII.
'Let Vanity adorn the marble tomb
With trophies, rhymes, and scutcheons of renown,
In the deep dungeon of some Gothic dome,
Where night and desolation ever frown.
Mine be the breezy hill that skirts the down;
Where a green grassy turf is all I crave,
With here and there a violet bestrown,
Fast by a brook, or fountain's murmuring wave;
And many an evening sun shine sweetly on my grave.

XVIII.
'And thither let the village swain repair;
And, light of heart the village maiden gay,
To deck with flowers her half-dishevel'd hair,
And celebrate the merry morn of May;
There let the shepherd's pipe the livelong day,
Fill all the grove with love's bewitching wo;
And when mild Evening comes with mantle gray,
Let not the blooming band make haste to go,
No ghosts nor spell my long and last abode shall know.

XIX.
'For though I fly to 'scape from fortune's rage,
And bear the scars of envy, spite, and scorn,
Yet with mankind no horrid war I wage,
Yet with no impious spleen my breast is torn;
For virtue lost, and ruin'd man, I mourn.
O man, creation's pride, heaven's darling child,
Whom nature's best, divinest gifts adorn,
Why from thy home are truth and joy exiled,
And all thy favourite haunts with blood and tears defiled!

XX.
'Along yon glittering sky what glory streams!
What majesty attends night's lovely queen;
Fair laugh our valleys in the vernal beams;
And mountains rise, and oceans roll between,
And all conspire to beautify the scene.
But, in the mental world, what chaos drear!

What forms of mournful, loathsome, furious mien!
O when shall Eternal Morn appear,
These dreadful forms to chase, this chaos dark to clear.

XXI.
'O thou, at whose creative smile, yon heaven,
In all the pomp of beauty, life, and light,
Rose from th' abyss; when dark Confusion, driven
Down down the bottomless profound of night,
Fled, where he ever flies thy piercing sight!
O glance on these sad shades one pitying ray,
To blast the fury of oppressive might,
Melt the hard heart to love and mercy's sway,
And cheer the wandering soul, and light him on the way.'

XXII.
Silence ensued: and Edwin raised his eyes
In tears, for grief lay heavy at his heart.
'And it is thus in courtly life (he cries)
That man to man acts a betrayer's part!
And dares he thus the gifts of Heaven pervert,
Each social instinct, and sublime desire! -
Hail poverty! if honour, wealth, and art,
If what the great pursue, and learn'd admire,
Thus dissipate and quench the soul's ethereal fire!'

XXIII.
He said, and turn'd away; nor did the sage
O'erhear, in silent orisons employ'd.
The youth, his rising sorrow to assuage,
Home as he hied, the evening scene enjoy'd:
For now no cloud obscures the starry void;
The yellow moonlight sleeps on all the hills;
Nor is the mind with startling sounds annoy'd,
A soothing murmur the lone region fills
Of groves, and dying gales, and melancholy rills.

XXIV.
But he from day to day more anxious grew,
The voice still seem'd to vibrate on his ear,
Nor durst he hope the Hermit's tale untrue;
For man he seem'd to love, and Heaven to fear;
And none speaks false, where there is none to hear.
'Yet can man's gentle heart become so fell!
No more in vain conjecture let me wear
My hours away, but seek the Hermit's cell;
'Tis he my doubt can clear, perhaps my care dispel.'

XXV.
At early dawn the youth his journey took,
And many a mountain pass'd, and valley wide,

Then reach'd the wild; where, in a flowery nook
And seated on a mossy stone, he spied
An ancient man: his harp lay him beside.
A stag sprung from the pasture at his call,
And, kneeling, lick'd the wither'd hand, that tied
A wreathe of woodbine round his antlers tall,
And hung his lofty neck with many a floweret small.

XXVI.
And now the hoary sage arose, and saw
The wanderer approaching: innocence
Smiled on his glowing cheek, but modest awe
Depress'd his eye, that fear'd to give offence.
'Who art thou, courteous stranger? and from whence?
Why roam thy steps to this abandon'd dale?'
'A shepherd-boy (the youth replied) far hence
My habitation; hear my artless tale;
Nor levity nor falsehood shall thine ear assail.

XXVII.
'Late as I roam'd, intent on Nature's charms,
I reach'd at eve this wilderness profound;
And, leaning where yon oak expands her arms,
Heard these rude cliffs thine awful voice rebound,
(For in thy speech I recognise the sound.)
You mourn'd for ruin'd man, and virtue lost,
And seem'd to feel of keen remorse the wound,
Pondering on former days, by guilt engross'd,
Or in the giddy storm of dissipation toss'd.

XXVIII.
'But say, in courtly life can craft be learn'd
Where knowledge opens, and exalts the soul?
Where Fortune lavishes her gifts unearn'd,
Can selfishness the liberal heart control?
Is glory there achieved by arts, as foul
As those which felons, fiends, and furies plan?
Spiders ensnare, snakes poison, tygers prowl;
Love is the godlike attribute of man.
O teach a simple youth this mystery to scan.

XXIX.
'Or else the lamentable strain disclaim,
And give me back the calm, contended mind;
Which, late exulting, view'd, in Nature's frame,
Goodness untainted, wisdom unconfined,
Grace, grandeur, and utility combined.
Restore those tranquill days, that saw me still
Well pleased with all, but most with human kind;
When Fancy roam'd through Nature's works at will,
Uncheck'd by cold distrust, and uninform'd of ill.'

XXX.
'Wouldest thou (the sage replied) in peace return
To the gay dreams of fond romantic youth,
Leave me to hide, in this remote sojourn,
From every gentle ear the dreadful truth:
For if my desultory strain with ruth
And indignation make thine eyes o'erflow,
Alas! what comfort could thy anguish soot,
Shouldst thou th' extent of human folly know.
Be ignorance thy choice, where knowledge leads to wo.

XXXI.
'But let untender thoughts afar be driven;
Nor venture to arraign the dread decree;
For know, to man, as candidate for heaven,
The voice of the Eternal said, Be free;
And this divine prerogative to thee
Does virtue, happiness, and heaven convey:
For virtue is the child of liberty,
And happiness of virtue; nor can they
Be free to keep the path who are not free to stray.

XXXII.
'Yet leave me not. I would allay that grief,
Which else might thy young virtue overpower;
And in thy converse I shall find relief,
When the dark shades of melancholy lower;
For solitude has many a dreary hour,
Even when exempt from grief, remorse, and pain:
Come often then; for, haply, in my bower
Amusement then, knowledge, wisdom thou may'st gain
If I one soul improve, I have not lived in vain.'

XXXIII.
And now, at length, to Edwin's ardent gaze
The Muse of history unrolls her page,
But few, alas! the scenes her art displays
To charm his fancy, or his heart engage,
Here Chiefs their thirst of power in blood assuage,
And straight their flames with tenfold fierceness burn:
Here smiling Virtue prompts the patriot's rage,
But lo, ere long, is left alone to mourn,
And languish in the dust, and clasp th' abandon'd urn.

XXXIV.
'Ah, what avails (he said) to trace the springs,
That whirl of empire the stupendous wheel!
Ah, what have I to do with conquering kings,
Hands drench'd in blood, and breasts begirt with steel!
To those, whom Nature taught to think and feel,

Heroes, alas! are things of small concern.
Could History man's secret heart reveal,
And what imports a heaven-born mind to learn,
Her transcripts to explore what bosom would not yearn!

XXXV.
'This praise, O Cheronean Sage, is thine.
(Why should this praise to thee alone belong!)
All else from Nature's moral path decline,
Lured by the toys that captivate the throng;
To herd in cabinets, and camps, among
Spoil, carnage, and the cruel pomp of pride;
Or chaunt of heraldry the drowsy song,
How tyrant blood, o'er many a region wide,
Rolls to a thousand thrones its execrable tide.

XXXVI.
'O who of man the story will unfold,
Ere victory and empire wrought annoy,
In that elysian age (misnamed of gold)
The age of love and innocence, and joy,
When all were great and free! man's sole employ
To deck the bosom of his parent earth;
Or toward his bower the murmuring stream decoy,
To aid the floweret's long-expected birth,
And lull the bed of peace, and crown the board of mirth.

XXXVII.
'Sweet were your shades, O ye primeval groves,
Whose boughs to man his food and shelter lent,
Pure in his pleasures, happy in his loves,
His eye still smiling, and his heart content.
Then, hand in hand, Health, Sport, and Labour went.
Nature supplied the wish she taught to crave.
None prowl'd for prey, none watch'd to circumvent,
To all an equal lot Heaven's bounty gave;
No vassal fear'd his lord, no tyrant fear'd his slave.

XXXVIII.
'But ah! th' Historic Muse has never dared
To pierce those hallow'd bowers: 'tis Fancy's beam
Pour'd on the vision of th' enraptured Bard,
That paints the charms of that delicious theme.
Then hail sweet Fancy's ray! and hail the dream
That weans the weary soul from guilt and wo!
Careless what others of my choice may deem,
I long where Love and Fancy lead to go,
And meditate on heaven; enough of earth I know.

XXXIX.
'I cannot blame thy choice (the Sage replied)

For soft and smooth are Fancy's flowery ways,
And yet even there, if left without a guide,
The young adventurer unsafely plays.
Eyes dazzled long by Fiction's gaudy rays,
In modest Truth no light nor beauty find.
And who, my child, would trust the meteor-blaze,
That soon must fail, and leave the wanderer blind,
More dark and helpless far, than if it ne'er had shined!

XL.
'Fancy enervates, while it soothes, the heart
And, while it dazzles, wounds the mental sight;
To joy each heightening charm it can impart,
But wraps the hour of wo in tenfold night.
And often, where no real ills affright,
Its visionary fiends, and endless train,
Assail with equal or superior might,
And thro' the throbbing heart, and dizzy brain,
And shivering nerves, shoot stings of more than mortal pain.

XLI.
'And yet, alas! the real ills of life
Claim the full vigour of a mind prepared,
Prepared for patient, long, laborious strife,
Its guide Experience, and Truth its guard.
We fare on earth as other men have fared;
Were they successful? Let not us despair.
Was disappointment oft their sole reward?
Yet shall their tale instruct, if it declare
How they have borne the load ourselves are doom'd to bear.

XLII.
'What charms th' Historic Muse adorn, from spoils,
And blood, and tyrants, when she wings her flight,
To hail the patriot Prince, whose pious toils
Sacred to science; liberty, and right,
And peace, through every age divinely bright
Shall shine the boast and wonder of mankind!
Sees yonder sun, from his meridian height,
A lovelier scene, than Virtue thus enshrined
In power, and man with man for mutual aid combined?

XLIII.
'Hail sacred Polity, by Freedom rear'd!
Hail sacred Freedom, when by Law restrain'd?
Without you what were man? A grovelling herd
In darkness, wretchedness, and want enchain'd.
Sublimed by you, the Greek and Roman reign'd
In arts unrivall'd: O, to latest days,
In Albion may your influence unprofaned
To godlike worth the generous bosom raise,

And prompt the Sage's lore, and fire the Poet's lays!

XLIV.
'But now let other themes our care engage,
For lo, with modest, yet majestic grace,
To curb Imagination's lawless rage,
And from within the cherish'd heart to brace,
Philosophy appears. The gloomy race
By Indolence and moping Fancy bred,
Fear, Discontent, Solicitude give place,
And Hope and Courage brighten in their stead,
While on the kindling soul her vital beams are shed.

XLV.
'Then waken from long lethargy to life,
The seeds of happiness, and powers of thought;
Then jarring appetites forego their strife,
A strife by ignorance to madness wrought.
Pleasure by savage man is dearly bought
With fell revenge, lust that defies control,
With gluttony and death. The mind untaught
Is a dark waste, where fiends and tempests howl;
As Phoebus to the world, is Science to the soul.

XLVI.
'And Reason now through Number, Time, and Space,
Darts the keen lustre of her serious eye,
And learns from facts compared, the laws to trace,
Whose long progression leads to Deity.
Can mortal strength presume to soar so high!
Can mortal sight, so oft bedimm'd with tears,
Such glory bear! - for lo, the shadows fly
From Nature's face; Confusion disappears,
And order charms the eyes, and harmony the ears.

XLVII.
'In the deep windings of the grove, no more
The hag obscene, and grisly phantom dwell;
Nor in the fall of mountain-stream, or roar
Of winds, is heard the angry spirit's yell;
No wizard mutters the tremendous spell,
Nor sinks convulsive in prophetic swoon;
Nor bids the noise of drums and trumpets swell,
To ease of fancied pangs the labouring moon,
Or chase the shade that blots the blazing orb of noon.

XLVIII.
'Many a long-lingering year, in lonely isle,
Stunn'd with th' eternal turbulence of waves,
Lo, with dim eyes, that never learn'd to smile,
And trembling hands, the famish'd native craves

O Heaven his wretched fare: shivering in caves,
Or scorch'd on rocks, he pines from day to day;
But Science gives the word; and lo, he braves
The surge and tempest, lighted by her ray,
And to a happier land wafts merrily away.

XLIX.
'And even where Nature loads the teeming plain
With the full pomp of vegetable store,
Her beauty, unimproved, is deadly bane;
Dark woods and rankling wilds, from shore to shore,
Stretch their enormous gloom; which to explore
Even Fancy trembles, in her sprightliest mood;
For there each eyeball gleams with lust of gore,
Nestles each murderous and each monstrous brood,
Plague lurks in every shade, and teams from every flood.

L.
"Twas from Philosophy man learn'd to tame
The soil by plenty to intemperance fed.
Lo, from the echoing axe, and thundering flame,
Poison and plague and yelling rage are fled.
The waters, bursting from their slimy bed,
Bring health and melody to every vale:
And, from the breezy main, and mountain's head,
Ceres and Flora, to the sunny dale,
To fan their glowing charms, invite the fluttering gale;

LI.
'What dire necessities on every hand
Our art, our strength, our fortitude require
Of foes intestine what a numerous band
Against this little throb of life conspire!
Yet Science can elude their fatal ire
A while, and turn aside Death's levell'd dart,
Sooth the sharp pang, allay the fever's fire,
And brace the nerves once more, and cheer the heart,
And yet a few soft nights and balmy days impart.

LII.
'Nor less to regulate man's moral frame
Science exerts her all-composing sway,
Flutters thy breast with fear, or pants for fame,
Or pines to Indolence and Spleen a prey,
Or Avarice, a fiend more fierce than they?
Flee to the shade of Academus' grove;
Where cares molest not, discord melts away
In harmony, and the pure passions prove
How sweet the words of truth breathed from the lips of Love.

LIII.

'What cannot Art and Industry perform,
When Science plans the progress of their toil!
They smile at penury, disease, and storm;
And oceans from their mighty mounds recoil,
When tyrants scourge, or demagogues embroil
A land, or when the rabble's headlong rage
Order transforms to anarchy and spoil,
Deep-versed in man the philosophic Sage
Prepares with lenient hand their frenzy to assuage.

LIV.
''Tis he alone, whose comprehensive mind,
From situation, temper, soil, and clime
Explored, a nation's various powers can bind
And various orders, in one form sublime
Of polity, that, 'midst the wrecks of time,
Secure shall lift its head on high, nor fear
Th' assault of foreign or domestic crime,
While public faith, and public love sincere,
And Industry and Law maintain their sway severe.

LV.
Enraptured by the Hermit's strain, the Youth
Proceeds the path of Science to explore.
And now, expanding to the beams of Truth,
New energies, and charms unknown before,
His mind discloses: Fancy now no more
Wantons on fickle pinion through the skies;
But fix'd in aim, and conscious of her power,
Sublime from cause to cause exults to rise,
Creation's blended stores arranging as she flies.

LVI.
Nor love of novelty alone inspires,
Their laws and nice dependencies to scan;
For, mindful of the aids that life requires,
And of the services man owes to man,
He meditates new arts on Nature's plan;
The cold desponding breast of Sloth to warm,
The flame of Industry and Genius fan,
And Emulation's noble rage alarm,
And the long hours of Toil and Solitude to charm.

LVII.
But she, who set on fire his infant heart,
And all his dreams, and all his wanderings shared,
And bless'd the Muse, and her celestial art,
Still claim th' Enthusiastic's fond and first regard
From Nature's beauties variously compared
And variously combined, he learns to frame
Those forms of bright perfection, which the Bard,

While boundless hopes and boundless views inflame,
Enamour'd consecrates to never-dying fame.

LVIII.
Of late, with cumbersome, though pompous show,
Edwin would oft his flowery rhyme deface,
Through ardour to adorn; but Nature now
To his experienced eye a modest grace
Presents, where Ornament the second place
Holds, to intrinsic worth and just design
Subservient still. Simplicity apace
Tempers his rage: he owns her charm divine,
And clear th' ambiguous phrase, and lops th' unwieldy line.

LIX.
Fain would I sing (much yet unsung remains)
What sweet delirium o'er his bosom stole,
When the great Shepherd of the Mantuan plains
His deep majestic melody 'gan roll:
Fain would I sing, what transport storm'd his soul,
How the red current throbb'd his veins along,
When, like Pelides, bold beyond control,
Gracefully terrible, sublimely strong,
Homer raised high to heaven the loud, th' impetuous song.

LX.
And how his lyre, though rude her first essays,
Now skill'd to sooth, to triumph, to complain,
Warbling at will through each harmonious maze,
Was taught to modulate the artful strain,
I fain would sing: - but ah! I strive in vain -
Sight from a breaking heart my voice confound -
With trembling step to join yon weeping train,
I haste, where gleams funereal glare around,
And, mix'd with shrieks of wo, the knells of death resound.

LXI.
Adieu, ye lays, that Fancy's flowers adorn,
The soft amusement of the vacant mind!
He sleeps in dust, and all the Muses mourn,
He, whom each Virtue fired! each Grace refined,
Friend, teacher, pattern, darling of mankind! -
He sleeps in dust, - Ah, how should I pursue
My theme! - To heart-consuming grief resign'd,
Here on his recent grave I fix my view,
And pour my bitter tears. - Ye flowery lays, adieu!

LXII.
Art thou, my
Gregory, for ever fled!
And am I left to unavailing wo!

When fortune's storms assail this weary head,
Where cares long since have shed untimely snow
Ah, now for comfort whither shall I go!
No more thy soothing voice my anguish cheers
Thy placid eyes with smiles no longer glow,
My hopes to cherish, and allay my fears -
'Tis meet that I should mourn: - flow forth afresh my tears.

9 781783 942237